Frank C. Gaylord:
Sculptures & New Drawings

A Lifetime Retrospective

May 20 – June 3, 2015

Curator's statement

I received a telephone call in 2014 with a modest query, "would SPA want to exhibit my new drawings?" "Why of course, I responded, but isn't it time to assemble a lifetime retrospective?" Frank and I compared calendars and decided on late May and June of 2015, to coincide with the year Frank turned 90 and to overlap with Memorial Day since one of his most widely known works is the "The Column," the Korean War Memorial on the National Mall in Washington, D.C.

Working with Frank, a group of artwork was selected, including sculptures, sculpture models, his new drawings, photograph albums, and some historic paintings (amidst protests that the older paintings from his teen years should not be in the show). The photograph albums included images of sculptures that had been commissioned sharing pages with sculptures that were outstanding, but that did not receive the selection committee's nod.

Widely considered as one of the great master sculptors, Frank Gaylord's work was sought out and highly regarded throughout his career.

Sue Higby
Executive Director, Studio Place Arts
Exhibit Curator and Editor

ISBN: 978-0-692-66691-3
Library of Congress Control Number: 2016905707

Photographs by Jack Rowell
Photograph on pages 4–5 by Sue Higby
Photograph on page 13 by Stefan Hard, *The Times Argus*
Design by Darryl Garland

Exhibit Presented by
Studio Place Arts
201 N Main Street
Barre, VT 05641
(802) 479-7069
www.studioplacearts.com

To obtain additional information on the exhibit, contact Studio Place Arts.

Frank C. Gaylord: Sculptures & New Drawings

A Lifetime Retrospective

May 20 – June 3, 2015

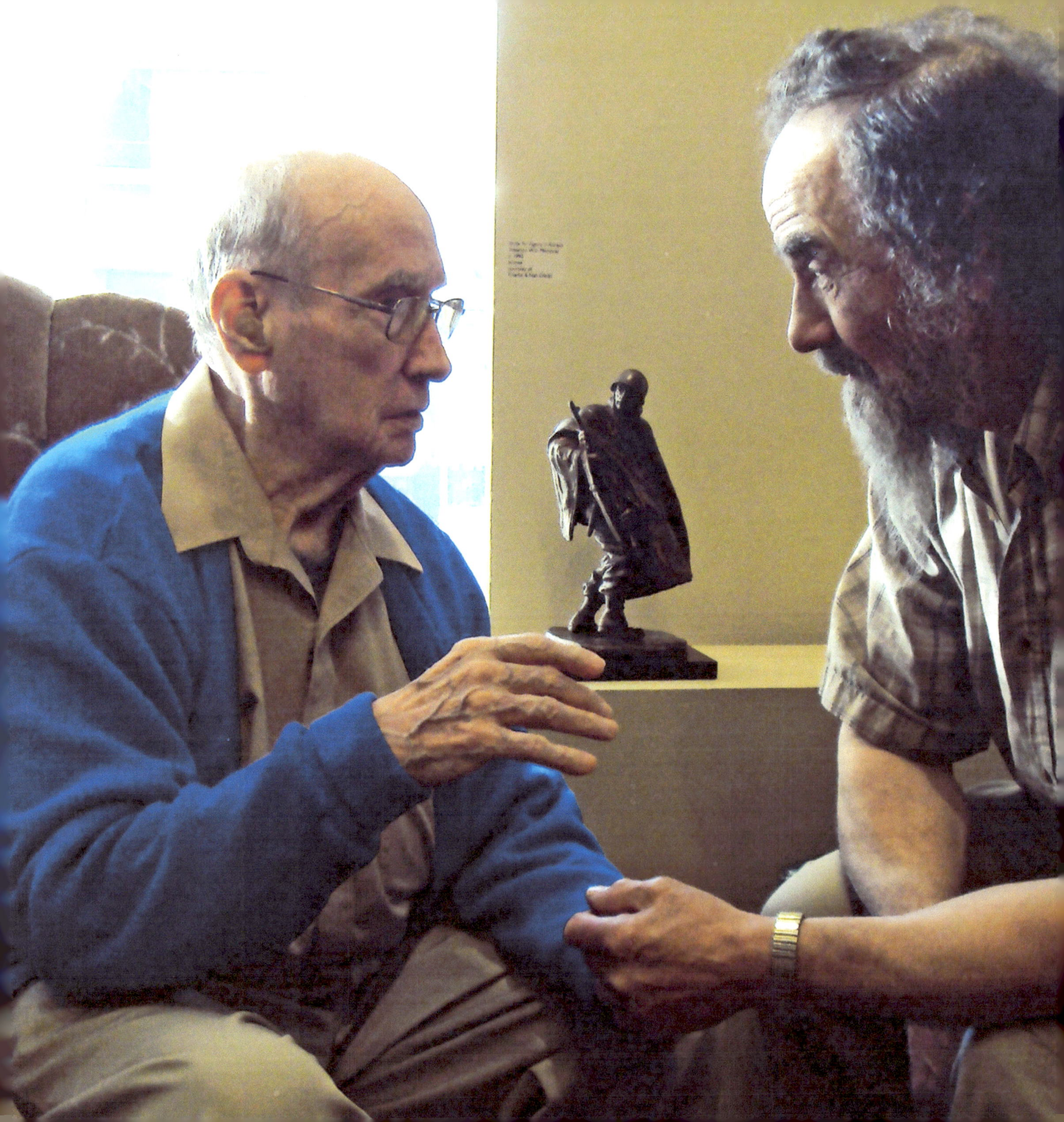

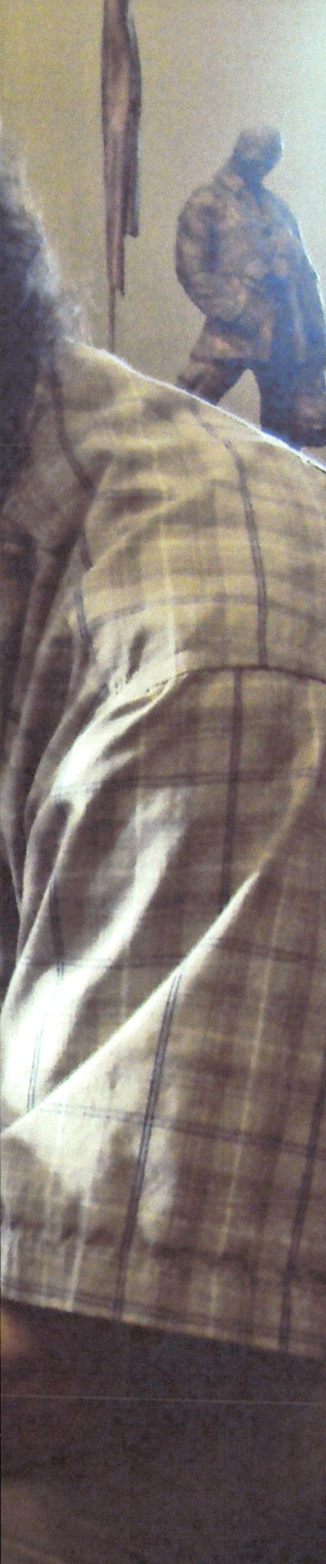

"An artist should not abdicate his imperative to circumscribe content in a meaningful way. Which is why all art should be answerable to its inner aspects and line is of little importance but the ethic the line describes, 'Ahhh!'"

— Frank C. Gaylord

Frank C. Gaylord speaks with Giuliano Cecchinelli at the show reception

Frank C. Gaylord: SPA's tribute to our 'national treasure'

By Steven M. Pappas, Editor, *The Times Argus,* May 21, 2015

There's an adage about what you can tell about a person from a handshake. Frank C. Gaylord's handshake speaks volumes.

At 90, his strong grip represents decades of sculpting, teasing concepts out of the hardest stones known to man, and making them — little by little — into art. His fortitude is an odd juxtaposition. He's soft-spoken but tough as hell. He is not the bulked-out, bicep-ripping man depicted in early photographs in his carving studio. His handshake today is somewhat unexpected, a surprise, like the breathtaking nuances hidden in plain sight among his hundreds — perhaps thousands — of works, most of them carved here in Barre.

He has defined an age of sculpting. In decades to come, young sculptors will undoubtedly wish they could have mentored under Gaylord.

That is the artist.

His hands have also pulled ripcords as a paratrooper, jumping into World War II combat zones. They have held in matrimony the hands of his loving wife, Mary, as well as their three children — John, Leanne and Victoria. He has shaken hands on commission deals to make some of the most recognizable public art in the world, including the National Korean War Veterans Memorial in Washington, D.C. He has honored the dead, the living and the fallen. Few hands have done so much.

A selection of Gaylord's elegant art went on display this week at Studio Place Arts. The retrospective of Gaylord's career includes 35 works, including models, sculptures, bas-reliefs, paintings and graphite drawings, as well as photo albums that will impress art students and aficionados alike.

Sue Higby, SPA's executive director, has admired Gaylord's work for years now. He used to participate in SPA's annual Stone Show, and he continued to attend the show a few times even after he had stopped presenting exhibits. Higby, her admiration for the man unconcealed, said it's important for the Granite City — and Vermont — to understand the magnitude of having someone of Gaylord's caliber.

"He's a national treasure," she said without equivocation.

On Tuesday afternoon, after giving Gaylord a sneak peak of the SPA show in his honor, Gaylord, sitting in a plush chair brought there in his honor, complimented Higby on her efforts.

"It's good," he said, humbly, and ever so quietly.

Higby thanked Gaylord, and choking up, said, "I had good material to work with."

Gaylord smiled modestly, and whispered, "Thank you."

The exchange went much farther than any handshake ever could.

HUMBLE BEGINNINGS

Frank Gaylord grew up with his younger sister, Ruth Ann, his parents and grandmother in Clarksburg, West Virginia, the county seat. "I was born on a street with doctors, lawyers and merchants," he recalled.

His father ran a wholesale grocery store. ("Two and half acres of dry goods. If it's good, we've got it.") His mother was a homemaker. Her family had ties going back to the nation's founding.

To keep little Frank busy and out from under foot, he recalled his grandmother giving him plastic molds into which he would press clay to make reliefs. "They sold (the kits) in dime stores."

But that was not enough. Gaylord, at around age 5 sitting at the kitchen table, watched his grandmother make clay animals for him — usually little dogs. But he wanted a menagerie.

"I asked her to make me some more, and she said she was too busy," he said. "You can make those yourself."

So he did. As he got more involved with making animals, he started carving soap — quickly learning how much material it actually took to make a full sculpture.

"I just started on one end making a lion, and by the time I got to the other side, there wasn't enough there to make a strong back end," Gaylord said. He began drawing figures onto the soap (as he would later learn sculptors do) to make the work more proportionate.

Gaylord attended public schools. He began bringing home some portraits he had drawn in school, and relatives and friends suggested the young man should do portraits of people around the community. He did so, his first commissioned works, "and the money was very good."

"I was still in school," he recalled during an interview from his apartment in Williamstown. "It was where I started."

Gaylord was initially interested in taxidermy, which, at that time, was done by sculpting plaster molds, with the animal skins pulled over them. "That looked good to me. It was a business," he said.

The war came along, and Gaylord became a paratrooper for two and a half years. While no specific stories were related, the experience abroad clearly had a profound impact on the man later in life. Gaylord served with the 17th Airborne and fought in the Battle of the Bulge. "I was very proud of my country," he recalled. "I did what I had to do."

The G.I. Bill allowed him to go where he wanted to go next. He ended up at the Carnegie Institute in Pittsburgh, which had both engineering and fine arts schools. "My father had told me, 'For God's sake, don't ever try to make a living in the arts,'" Gaylord recalled, because "it's suffering all the time."

By happenstance, the sculpture department was in the basement of one of the buildings, near the school's library.

"That's where I met a fella named Rodin," he said.

Ultimately, that led to a broader interest in fine arts than taxidermy, "so I stuck with it, against father's wishes," he said.

He met Mary there, married, and then eventually transferred to Temple University's Tyler School of Art, where he knew the dean was an accomplished sculptor. That dean was his first mentor, pushing Gaylord to "find my own way. … That was what changed my direction."

GETTING STARTED

Another Temple professor also saw Gaylord's potential, urging him to push himself outside the realm of the known, taught and practiced.

After school, the Gaylords lived in Philadelphia. While there, Frank realized most of the Temple graduates went on to become teachers. He was not interested. "I was determined I was not going to do that," he said. "I wanted to be creative."

So he wrote letters to communities with quarries all across the country — Alabama, Indiana and Vermont. Gaylord was determined to work with stone, doing carving.

In 1951, Mac Durnovich of E.J. Batchelder Co. in Barre hired Gaylord. So he and Mary moved to Vermont. He knew the community's reputation, its rich ethnic heritage, and its renowned craftsmanship. He said he knew he could learn here.

"I learned to carve. That is what I came here to do," he said, adding that he cut stone, or quarried, for a year, but after carving stone once, "that's all I wanted to do after that." He did religious figures that appeared on monuments. He is not a religious man, but he appreciates the beauty of religious imagery. In short order, his reputation for more intricate work caught up with him. People wanting designs they had seen Gaylord carve asked their dealers for him to do their final resting places, as well.

"Word had gotten around," he said. "I didn't just do the industry work."

He moved through the ranks to larger, local granite companies, eventually working with his other mentor, Bruno Sarzanini at Rock of Ages.

Gaylord stayed there three years. He carved the staples: sacred hearts, lilies, Christ figures and more. But Gaylord understood anatomy, and he could make a face look more like a face. Some of the other carvers were not as good, and it was not cost-effective for them to spend extra time on gravestones.

"Sarzanini left a good impression on me. He was a fine carver. There was nothing that he couldn't do," Gaylord said. "But he was not interested in creativity. He was interested in what the manufacturers wanted the sculptors to be interested in. (He'd say) 'We do it in granite, that is the best there is.'"

But Gaylord was not buying it. He was not satisfied with that answer.

"The best there is is the guy who designed the damn thing," he said. "He's the master … I wanted to be that guy."

ON HIS OWN

Gaylord left Rock of Ages, and rented studio space downtown, venturing out on his own.

"I made 80 dollars the first day, and 100 dollars the next day," he recalled. "That was a lot of money back then. I couldn't believe it. … I started making real money."

With every new request for portrait sculptures, Gaylord was able to use his creativity, and he began to venture out on his own, even hiring other, younger sculptors to work with him.

He sought more commission work, often putting forth his concept for models as proposals to win commission committees.

It paid off.

"Bosses at Rock of Ages said, 'He's a damn fool; he doesn't know what he's doing," Gaylord said. "I made them look like damn fools because I was a success."
It did not take long for his reputation to spread beyond Vermont. The work came fast and furiously.

He worked with local sculptors — many of whom he mentored; a few who sought their own path. His work ethic was firm, his standards were high, his attitude toward the work was uncompromising, building him a legion of detractors.

But his success surpassed his personnel issues. The respect for his talent transcended professional jealousies. Gaylord won commissions across North America.

"Eventually, I went on to public art," he said. "It grew to Army, Navy, the military, and doing more creative things."

Gaylord was ahead of his time. Some of his rejected works centered on sexuality or race — passed over not because they weren't beautiful, but, rather, because commission committees did not feel the public was ready for Gaylord's suggestive images. (Committees, Gaylord complains, are like camels, or "horses built by committee.")

He also did religious work, too. In fact, his favorite sculpture is one depicting a Spanish Christ, slightly more abstract, with hands crossed before him.

"That's my best work," Gaylord said.

The most well-known commission came in 1990 with the American Battle Monuments Commission selecting him to be the sculptor of the National Korean War Veterans Memorial in Washington, D.C. Other monuments created by Gaylord include the Firemens Memorial (Eugene, Ore.), Doctor Ashbel Smith (Baytown, Tex.), the Policemen's Memorial (Jacksonville, Fla.), the Toledo Mudhens Monument (Toledo, Ohio) and the National Little League Monument (Williamsport, Pa.).

Gaylord also has been awarded an honorary doctorate from Norwich University, as well as the Vermont Council on the Arts Governor's Award in 2003.

The SPA exhibit goes a bit further. It shows commission works done for sports, religion, history, memorials, and even rejected proposals. It is the first retrospective of Gaylord's distinguished career.

"It's wonderful to see it together," he said.

THE LAWSUIT

For a decade, Gaylord and the U.S. government have been at odds over part of his most noted success.

An image of soldiers walking on patrol as part of the Korean War national monument was used on a postage stamp without Gaylord's permission. (He heard about it when a fellow mourner congratulated him at a funeral.) He got a lawyer (and then another lawyer) and sued, taking the issue to court three times. Eventually, the U.S. Postal Service agreed with Gaylord and his business partner, John Triano of Northfield, who is also his son in law. A settlement, in the hundreds of thousands of dollars, is currently pending. The check is allegedly in the mail, Gaylord said.

The case has become a benchmark for American artists, who feel they need protection against copyright infringement of their images being used without permission.

The battle over artist's rights and government oversight has changed Gaylord at his core, however.

"I used to be patriotic," he said by way of explanation. "I was in combat, mortal combat. … I was carried away for love of country and so forth. … (This lawsuit caused me) to lose my love for my country."

Gaylord said the lawsuit should not diminish the ever-popular monument. "That was a love of military (and brothers in arms)," he said. "It does not have to be about a love of country."

He is somewhat bitter, and intolerant of the news he hears on television. But he admits he's too old now to really care all that much.

In the end, Gaylord said, "It will not matter. It will all be here long after I am gone."

COMMUNITY

Barre has been Gaylord's home longer than any other place.

He has made scores of friends here, and he has been an integral part of the granite industry's heyday. Many of his colleagues now rest in Hope Cemetery, surrounded by the very work that made them all famous.

"I love Barre," he said. "It will always be my home."

He and Mary, who died in 2003, made the Granite City theirs. There were social gatherings, card games, trips, tennis, golf and more. Gaylord keenly remembers businesses up and down Main Street with fond memories, faces long gone, hijinks whose laughs are now distant memories. (Many of Gaylord's current graphite works, done since 2013, are depictions of those feelings and times; one honors Mary outright.)

So it is with fondness and pride, sitting at SPA on Tuesday afternoon, that Gaylord took in this collection of his works – the sum of the parts of his life's work. Some he remembered well; others were lost to him, but he recognized the craftsmanship as his own.

With Higby refreshing his memory as to the show's extended hours, and the reception tonight, where Gaylord will once again take center stage in the plush chair, the sculptor nodded his approval. Expected to attend are the next generations of local sculptors — many who have long admired the man and his art.

"He's the best," Higby said. "I'm not just saying it. It will be true for the ages."

Frank C. Gaylord will live on for all time as one of the best American sculptors there ever was, Higby said.

Hands down.

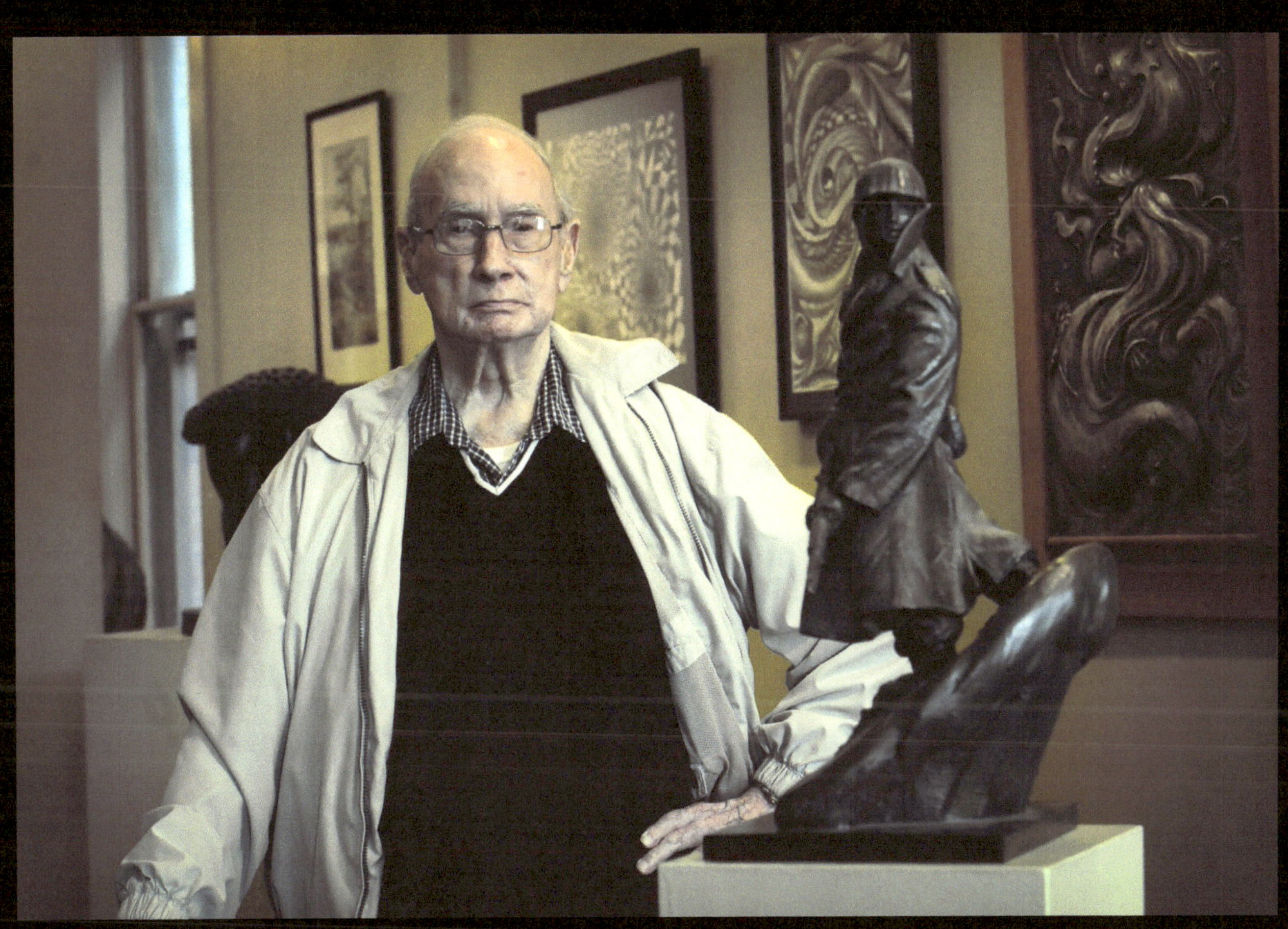

Frank C. Gaylord visits his exhibit at Studio Place Arts.

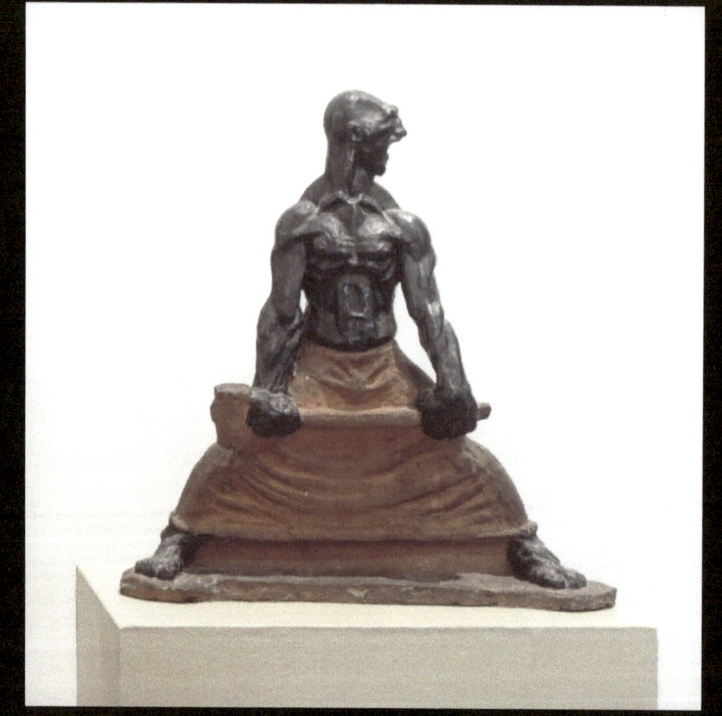

Study for John Henry 1981
clay
Collection of The Waskowmium
11.5"w x 11"l x 4"d

John Henry 1986
resin
Collection of The Vermont Historical Society
23.5"h x 28"w x 4"d

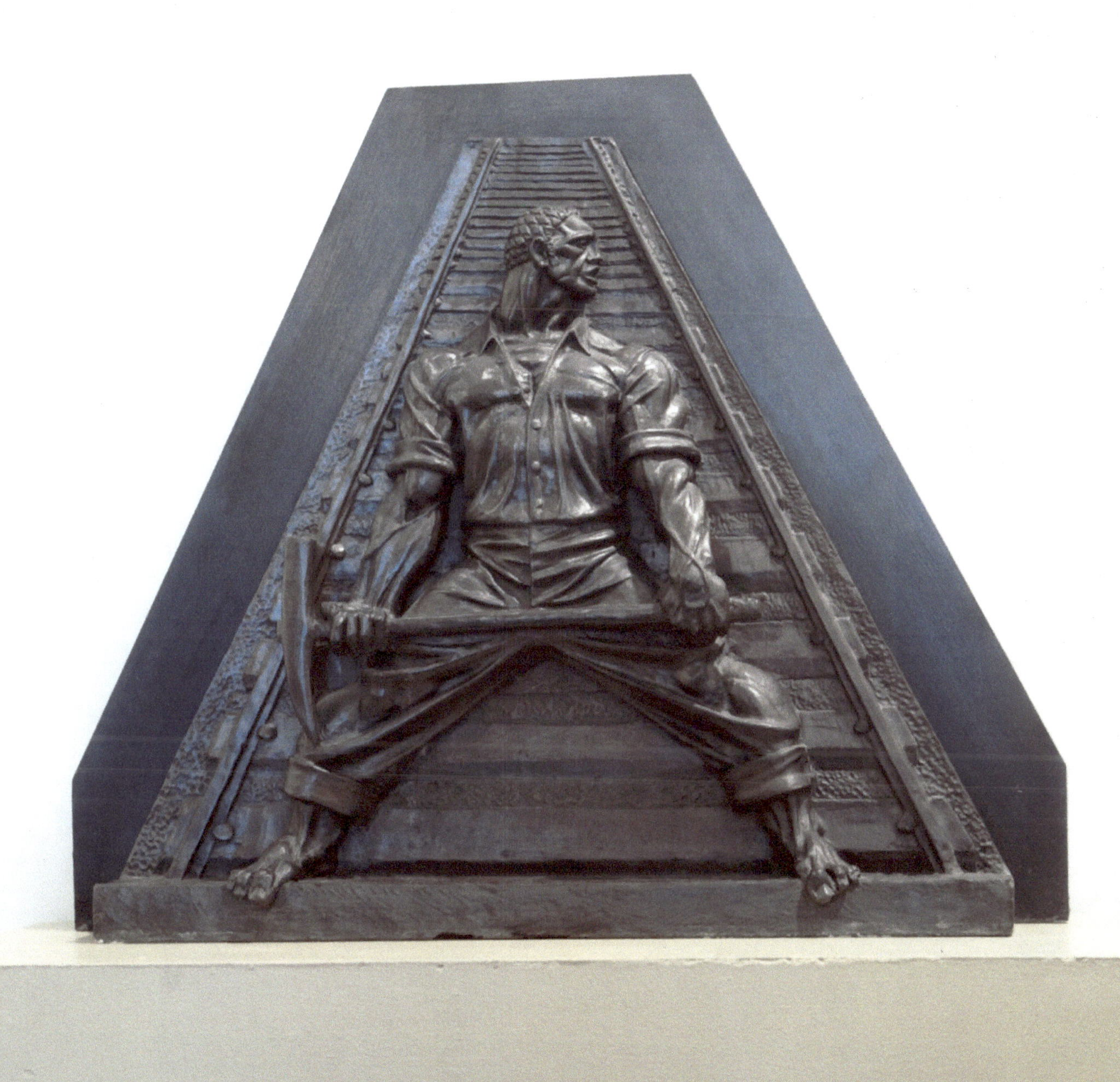

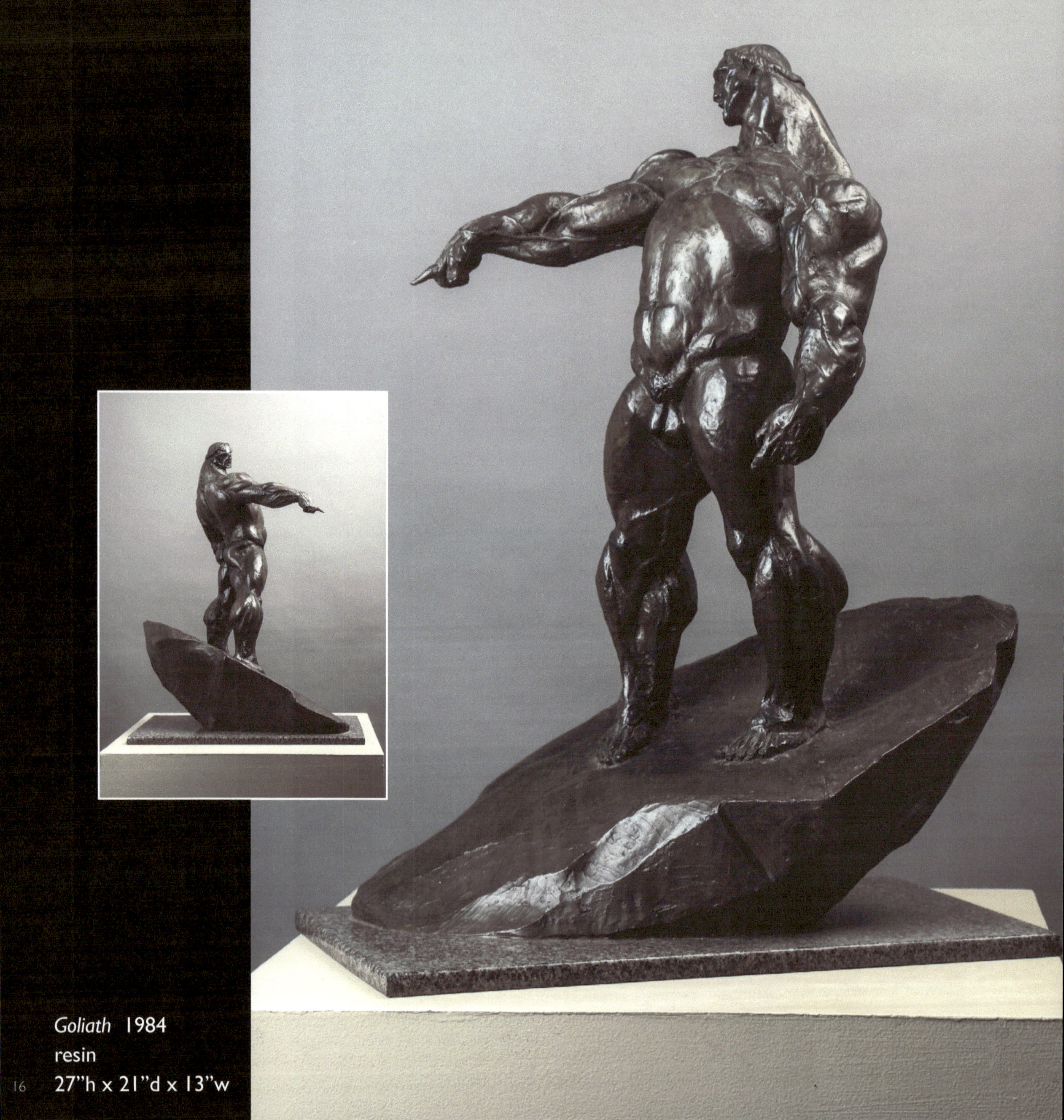

Goliath 1984
resin
27"h x 21"d x 13"w

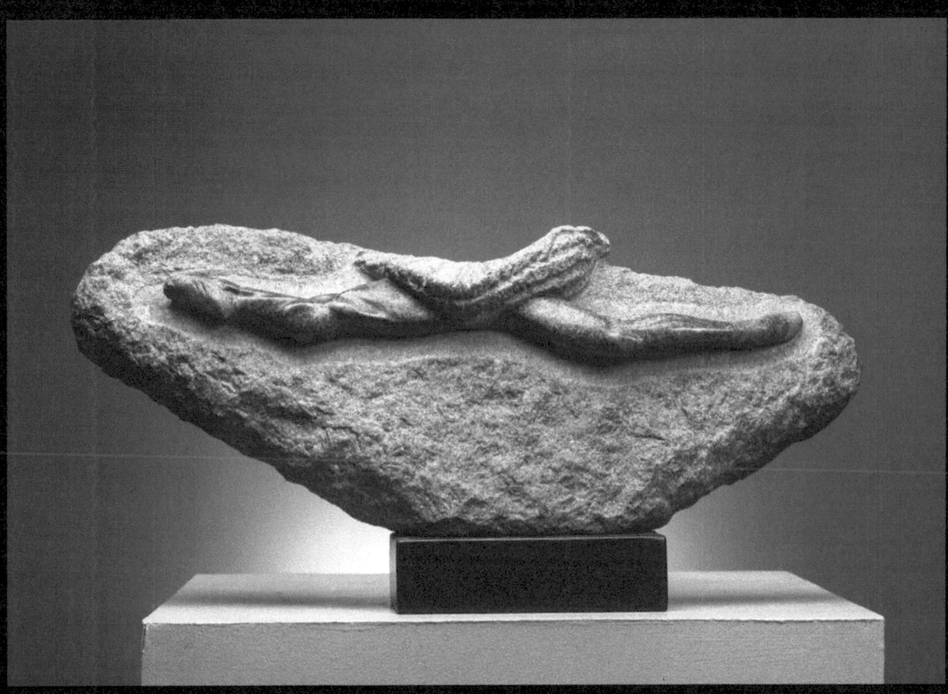

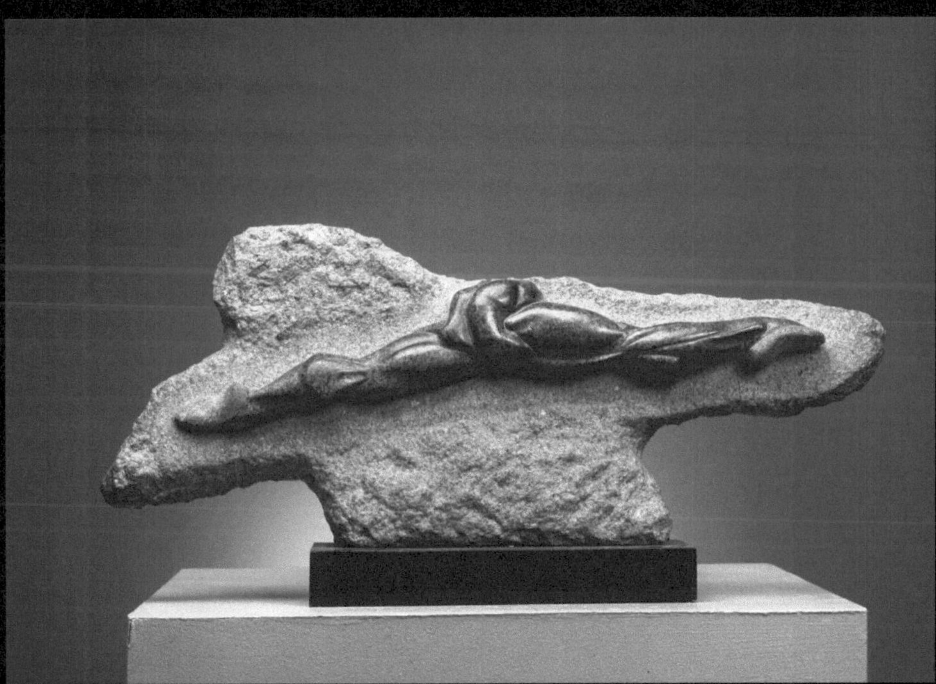

Grand Jeté Féminin 1982
pink granite
10"h x 27"w x 4.5"d

Grand Jeté Masculin 1983
pink granite
12"h x 27.5"w x 4"d

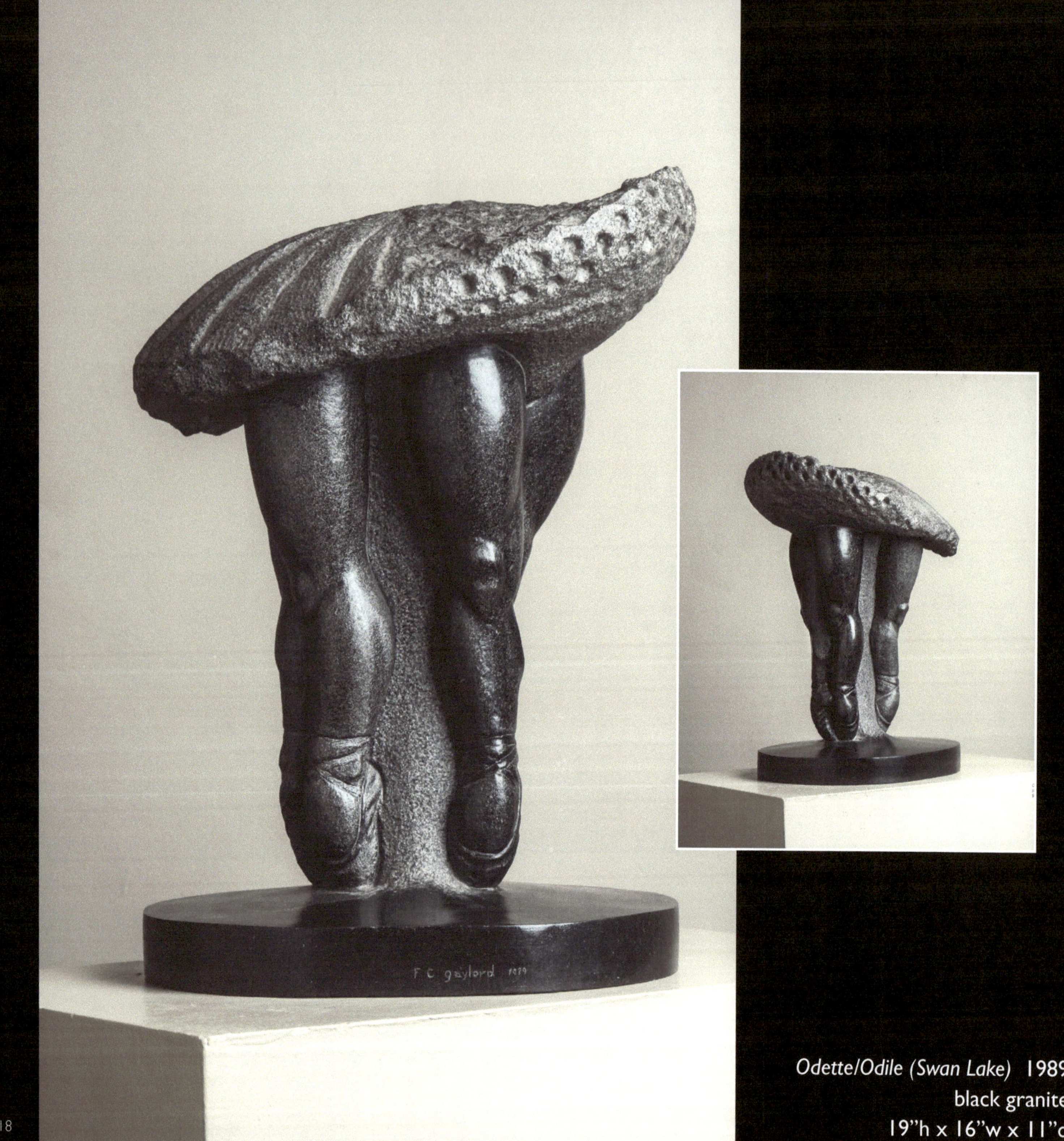

Odette/Odile (Swan Lake) 1989
black granite
19"h x 16"w x 11"d

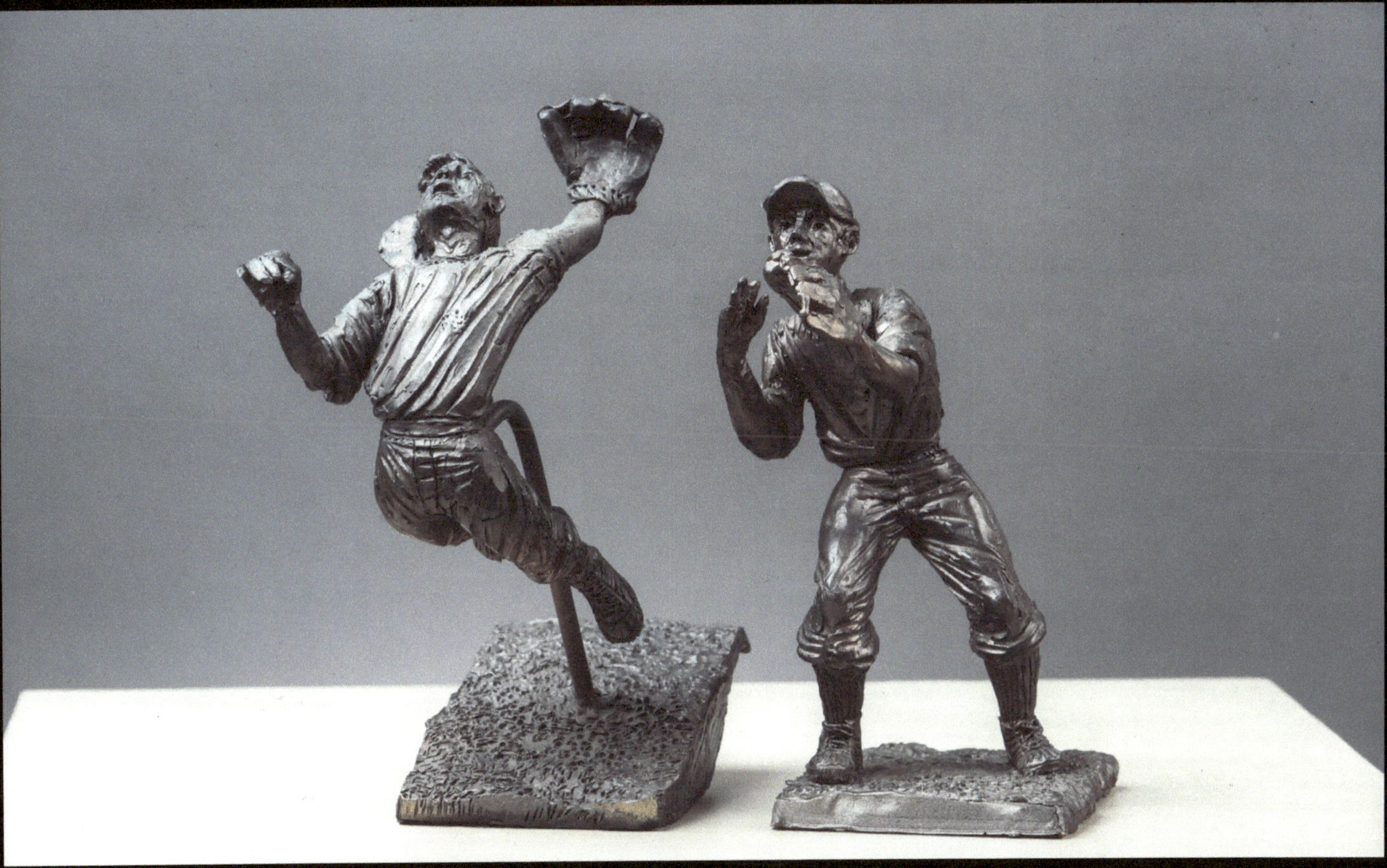

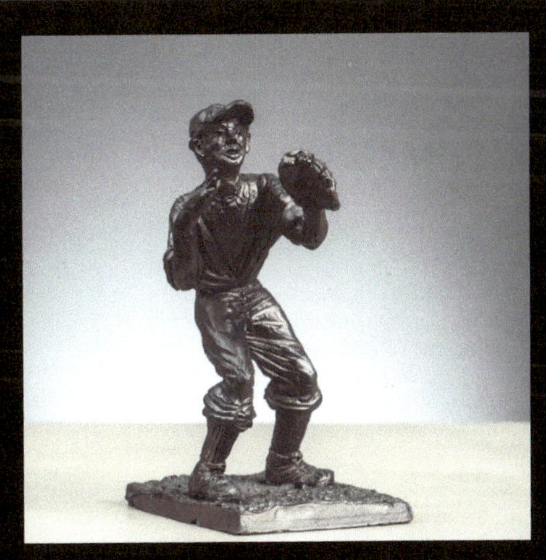
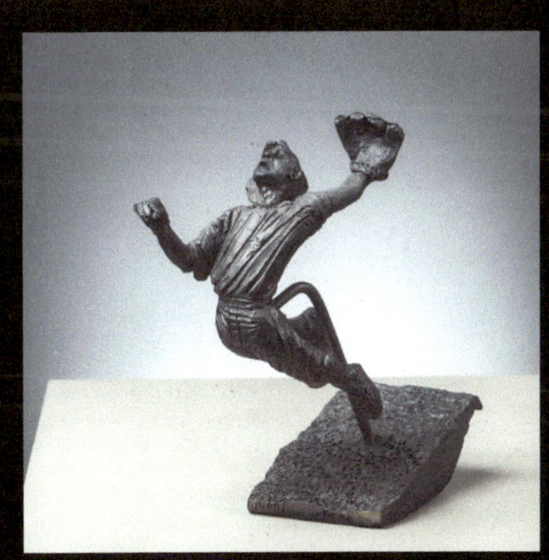

Study for "I Got It" (Toledo, Ohio) 1998
sculpey
10.5" h x10"d x 6"w (fly ball)
10.5"h x 10"d x 5.5"w (figure on ground)

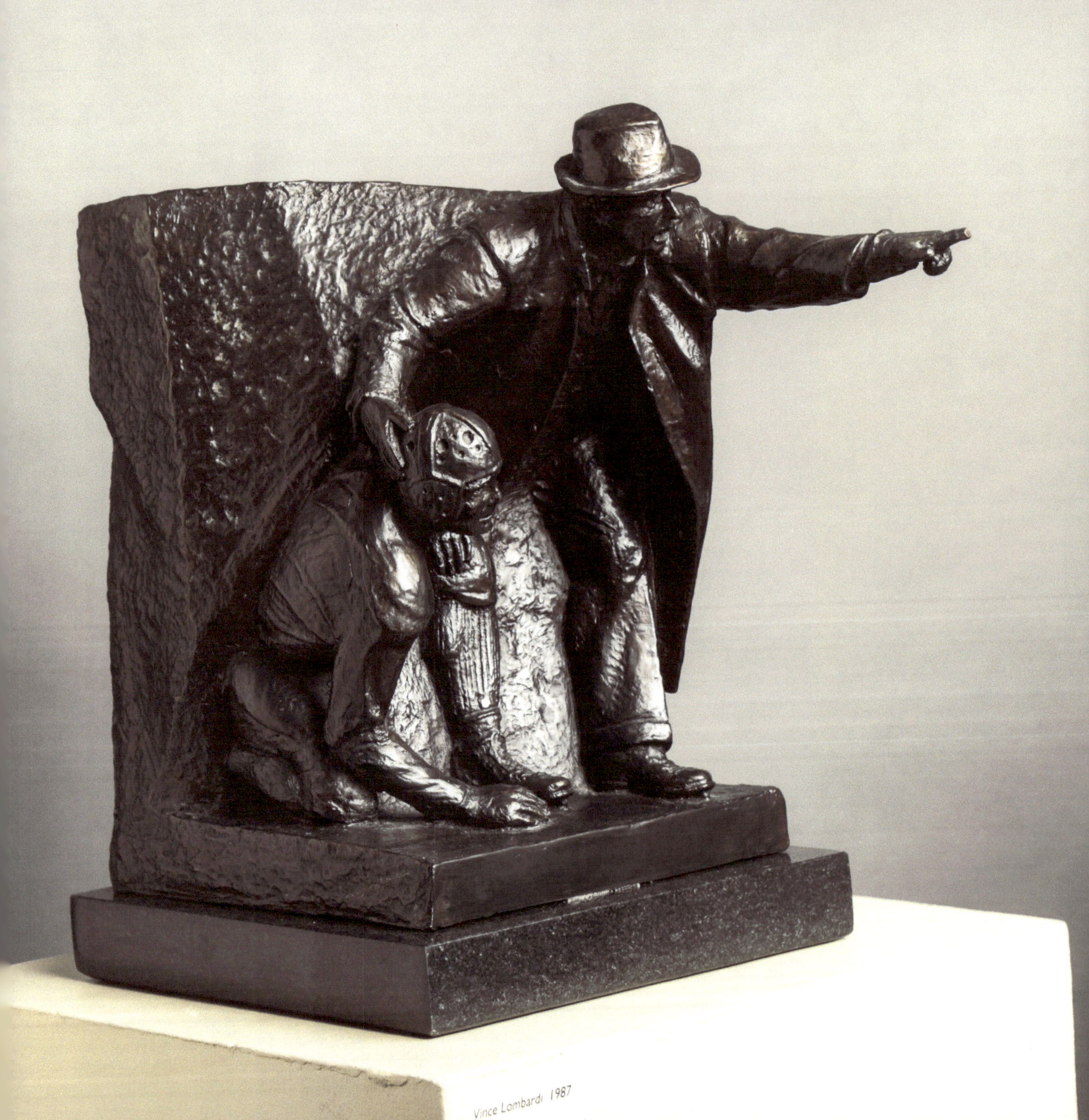

Vince Lombardi 1987

Vince Lombardi 1987
bronze
14"h x 9.25"w x 9.5"d

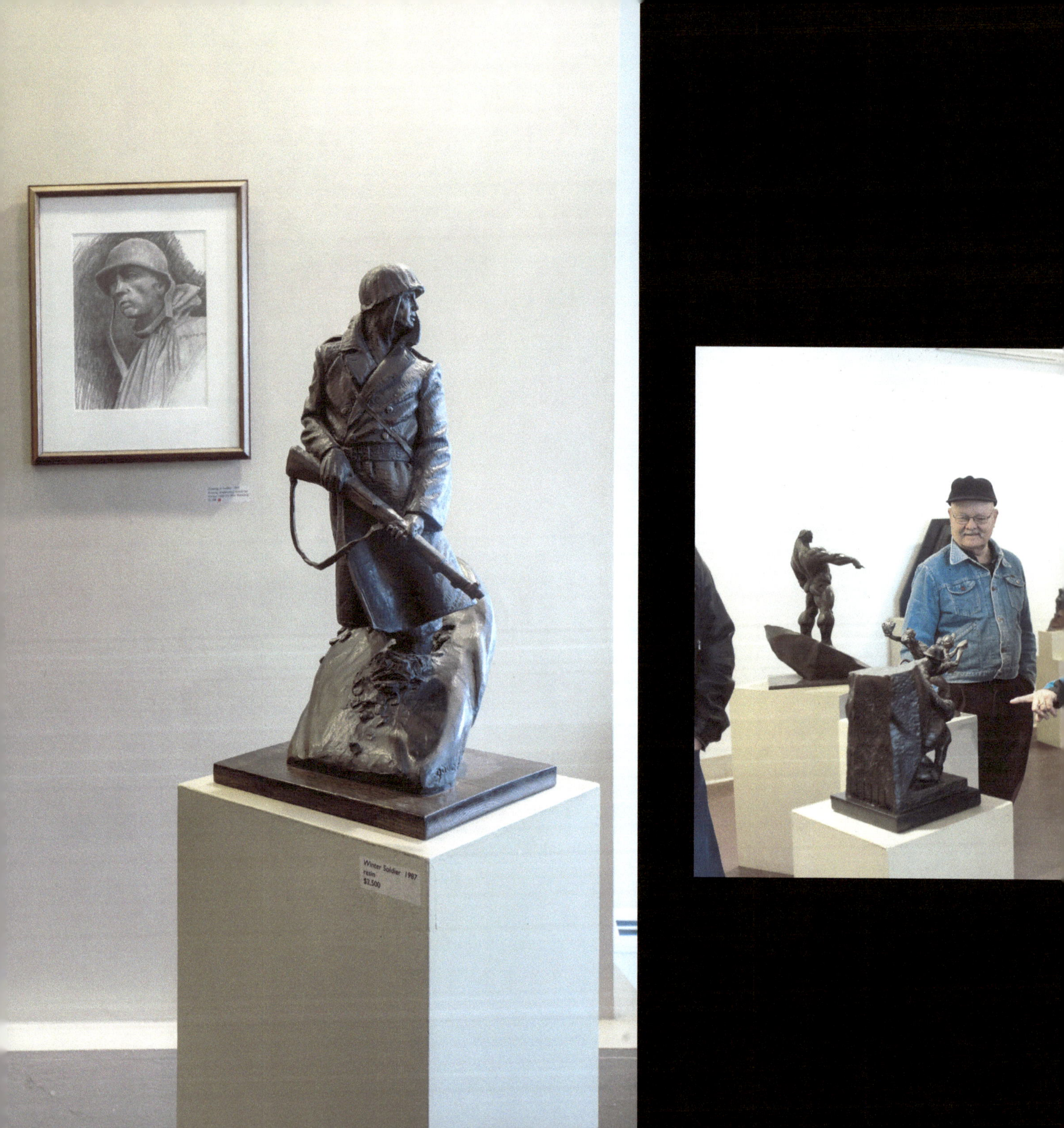
Winter Soldier 1987
resin
$2,500

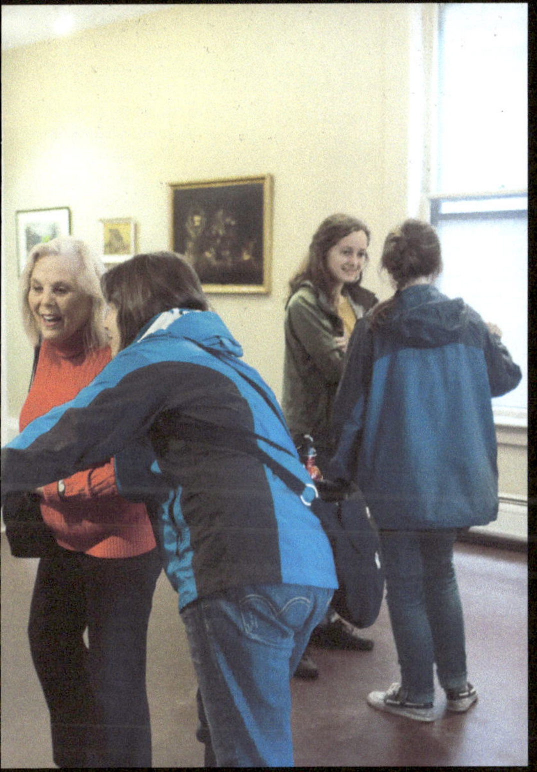

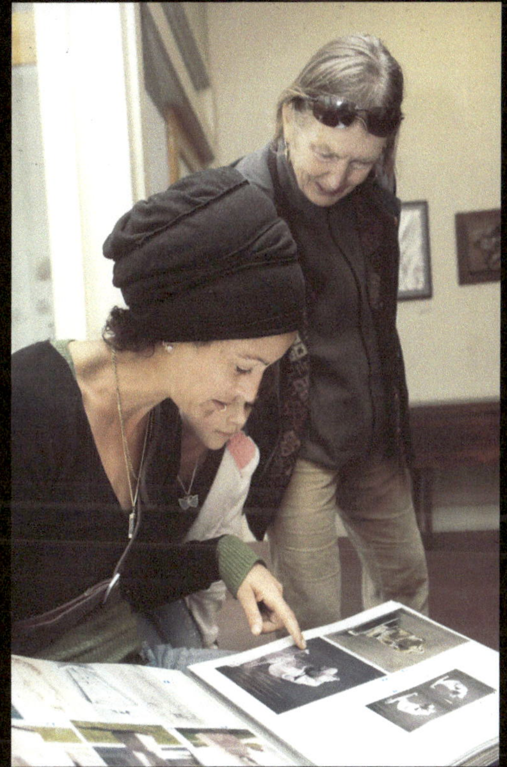

Green Mountain Boy 1981
resin
19.25"h x 9"w x 15"d

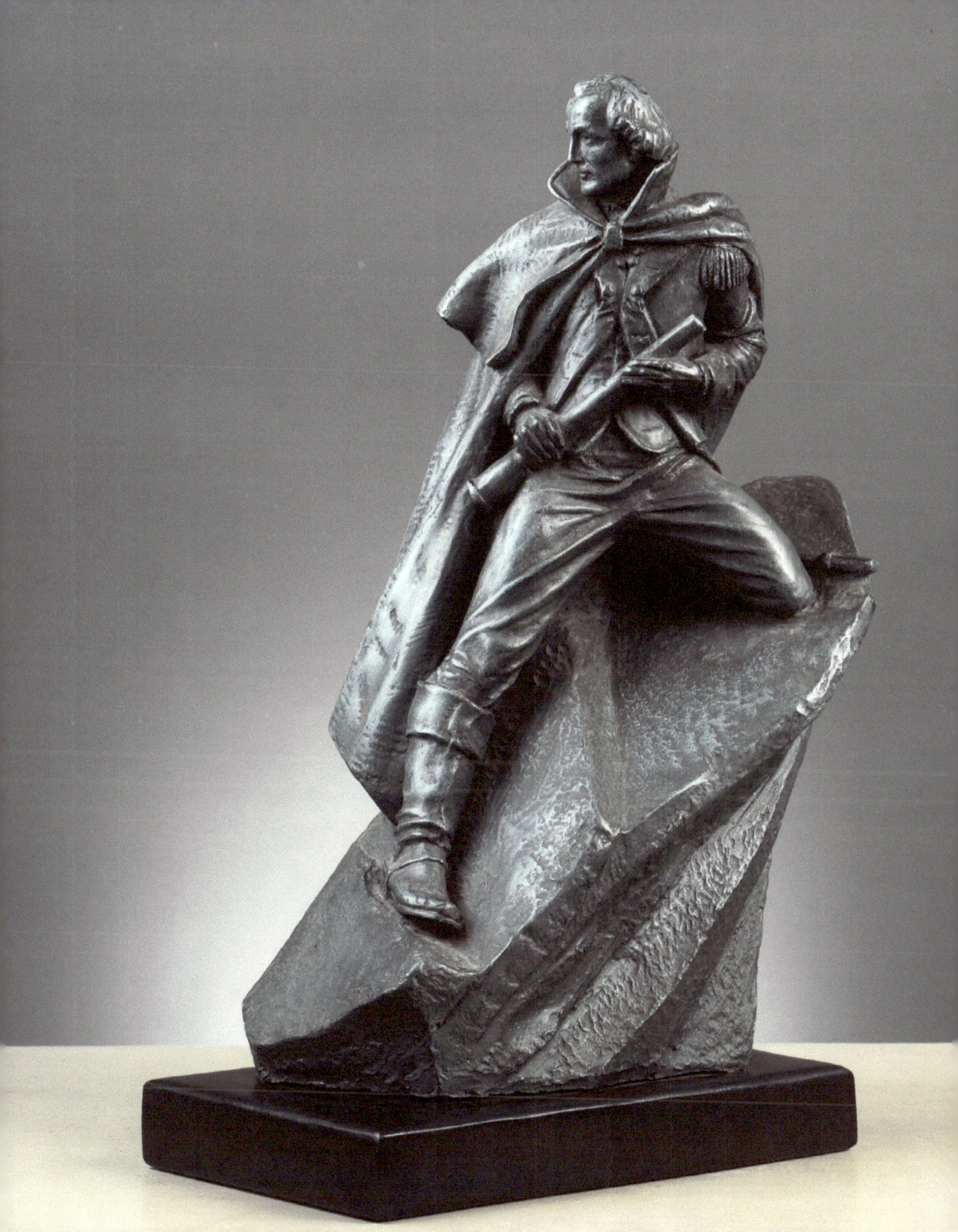

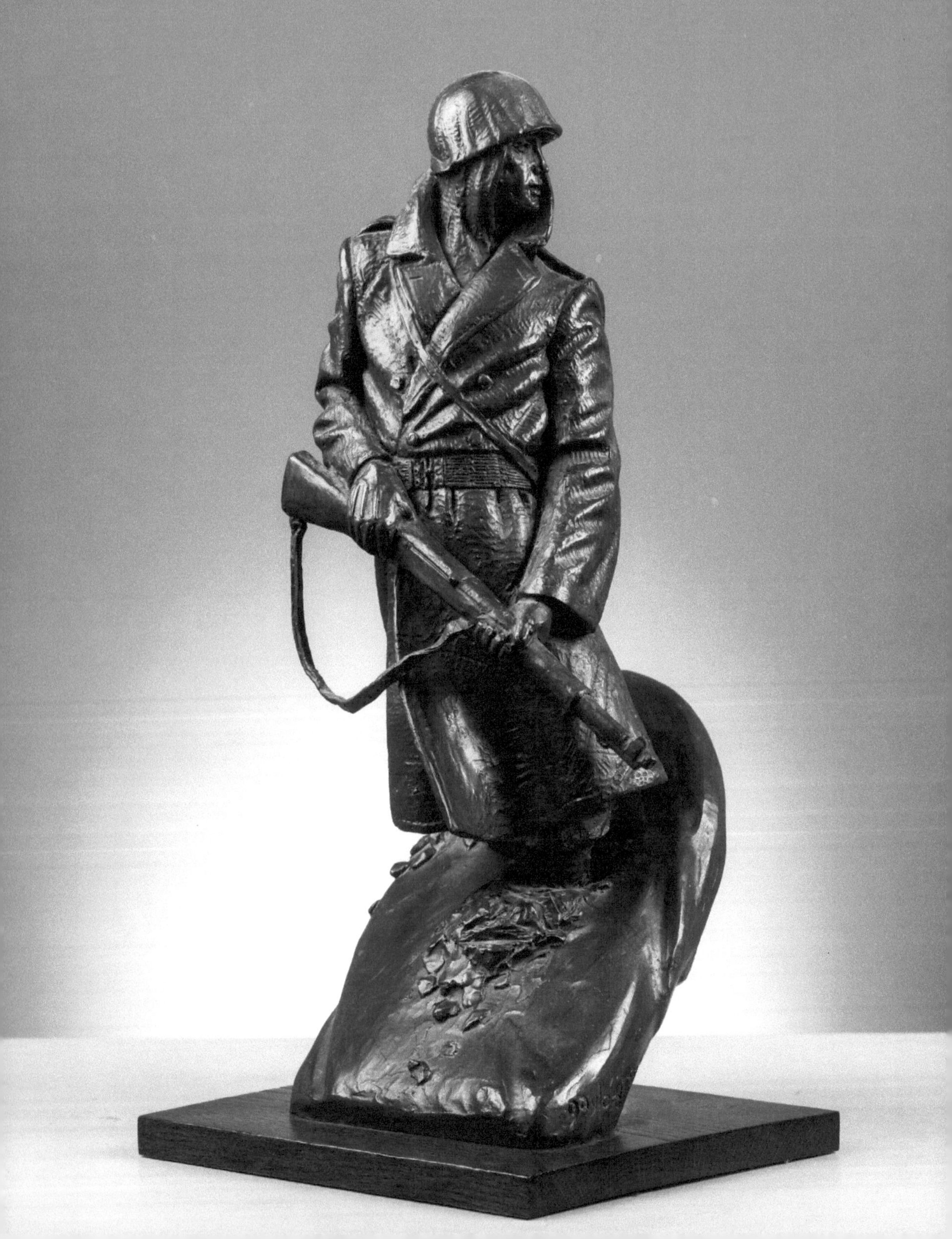

Winter Soldier 1987
resin
19.75"h x 8.5"w x 12.5"d

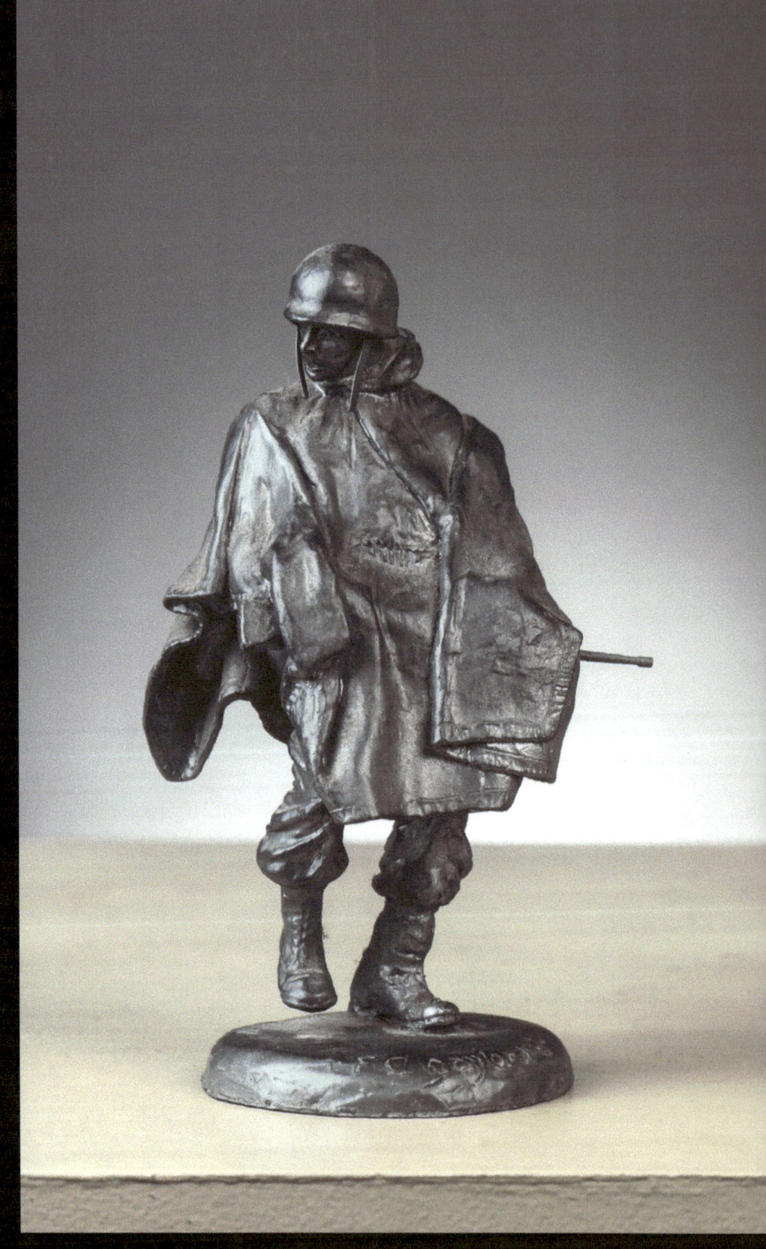

Study for Figure in Korean Veterans War Memorial c. 1990
plaster
8.5"h x 5.5"w x 4.5"d

Study for John Erdman Figure in Korean Veterans War Memorial c. 1990
bronze
Collection of Charlie & Nan Dindo
12"h x 6.5"w x 6"d

Model for Al Noyes Figure in Korean Veterans War Memorial
c. 1990
bronze
Collection of Bill & Diane Noyes
10.5"h x 3.5"w x 3.75"d

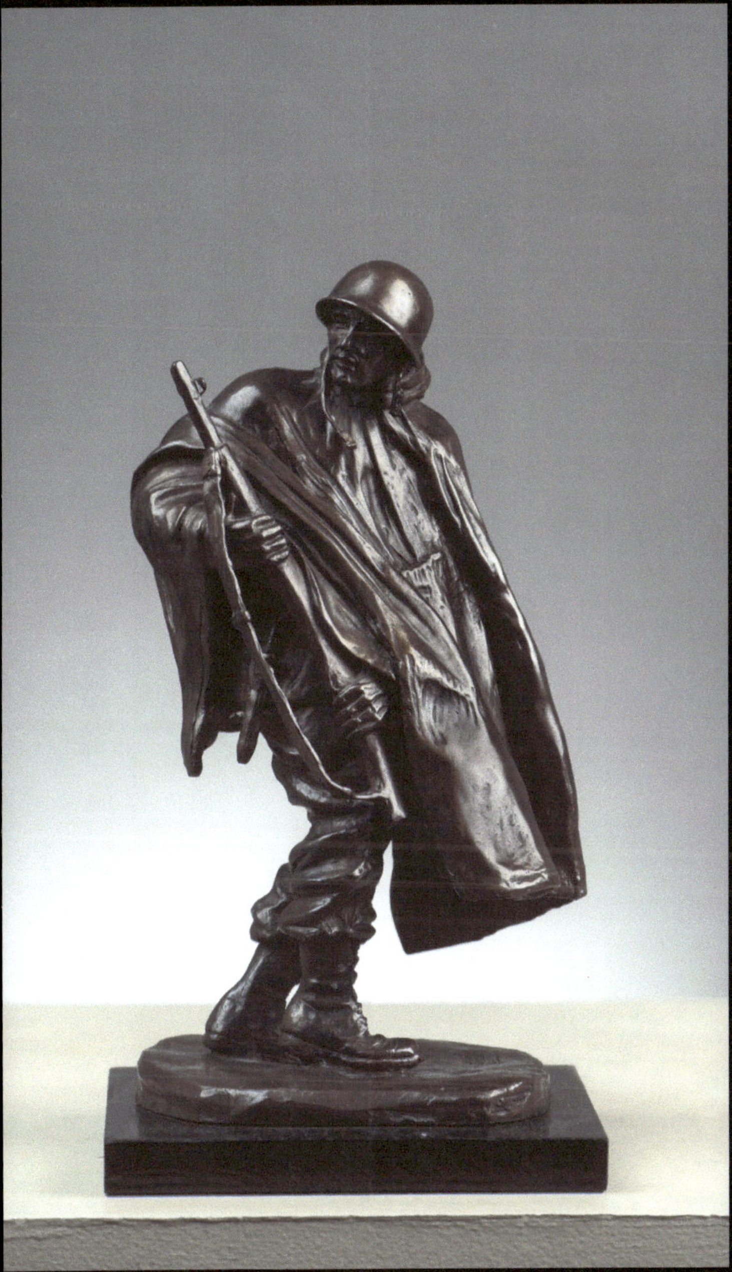

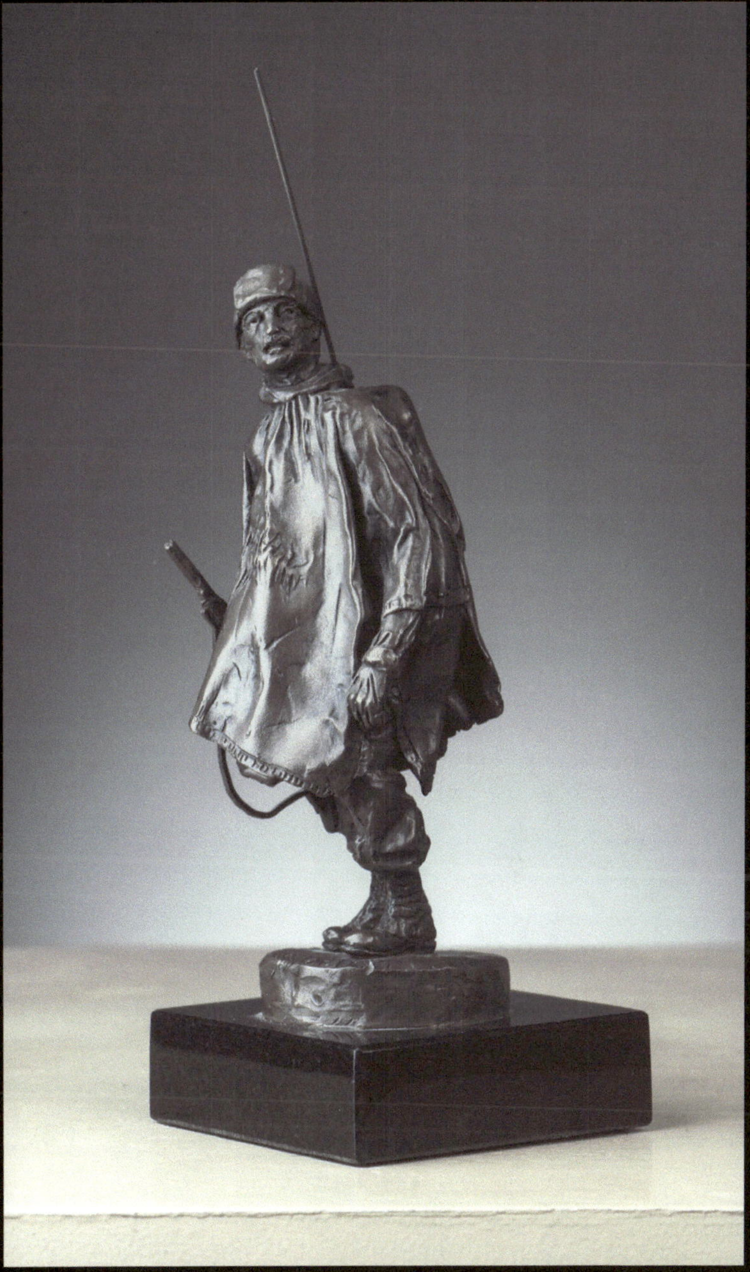

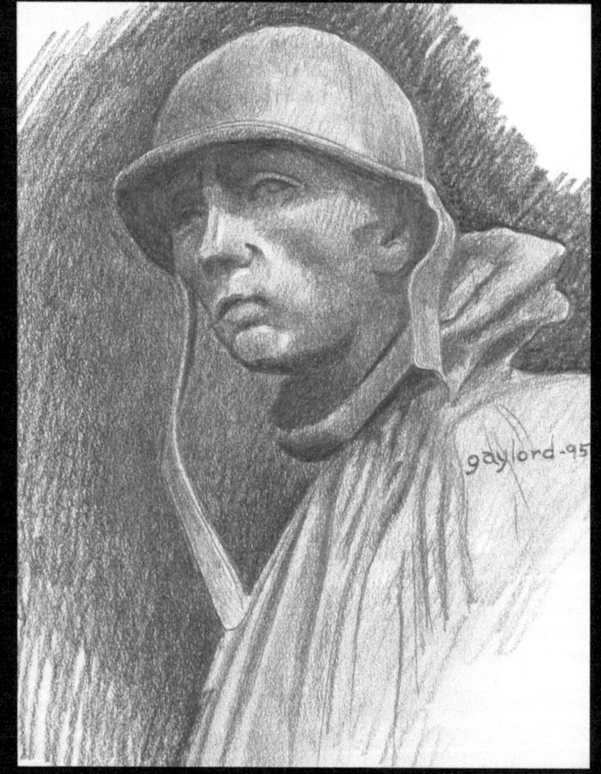

Drawing of Soldier 1995
drawing, preparatory sketch
for Korean Veterans War Memorial
Collection of The Waskowmium
13.25" x 10.25"

Deliverance
Bronze
Collection of Giuliano Cecchinelli
22"h x 12"w x 8"d

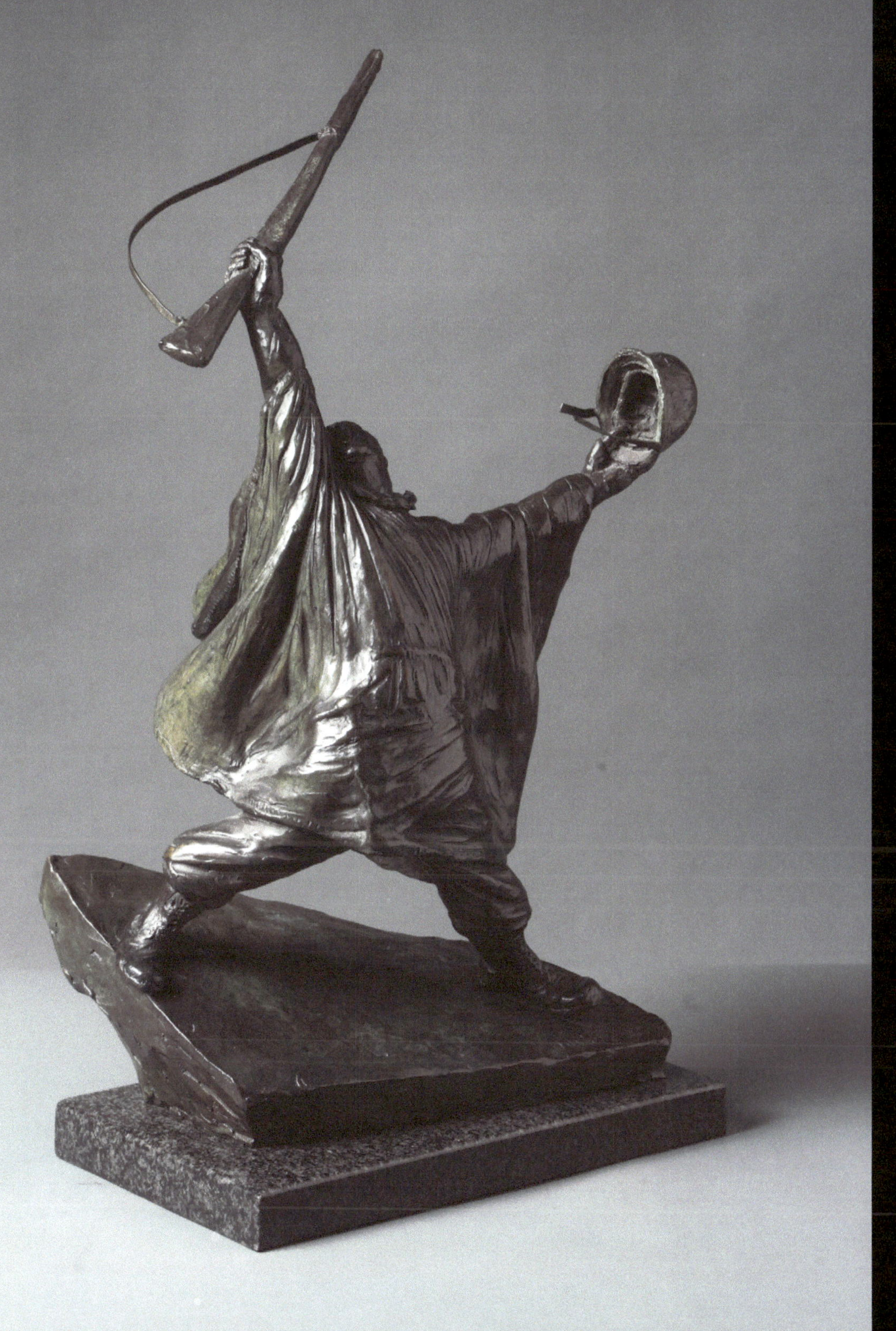

The Firemen 1990
sculpey
32.5"h x 10.25"w x 4.75

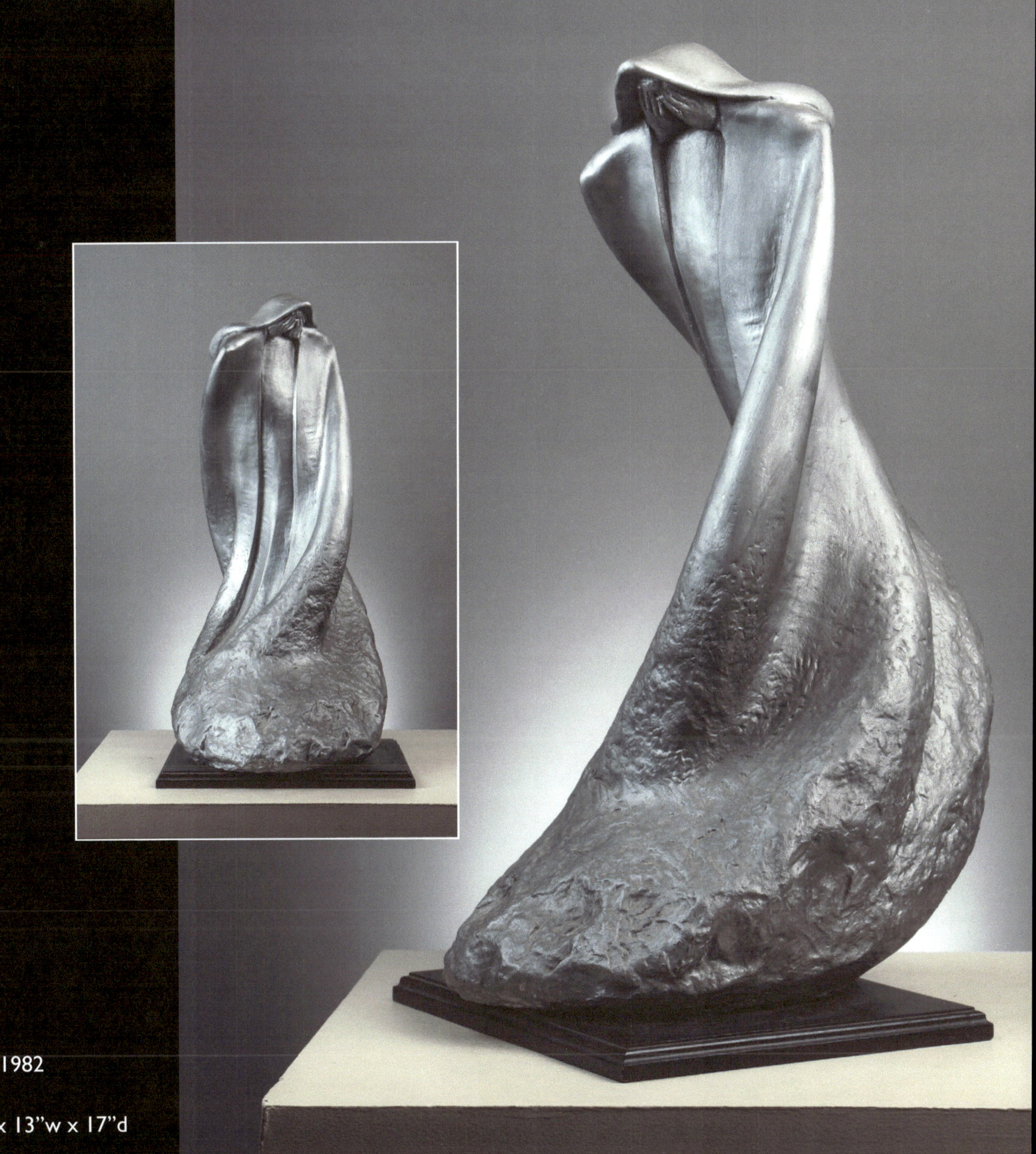

Grief 1982
resin
27"h x 13"w x 17"d

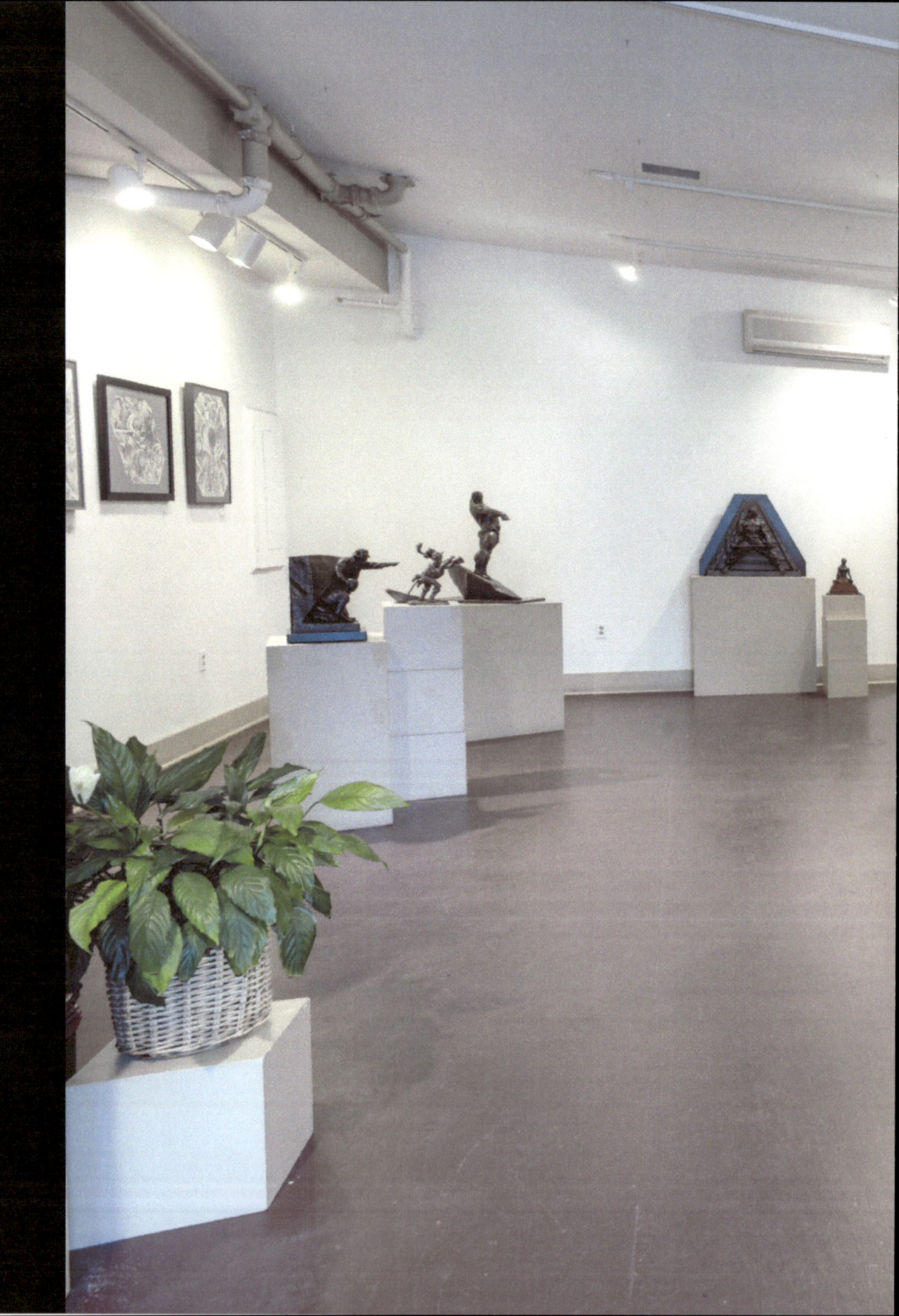

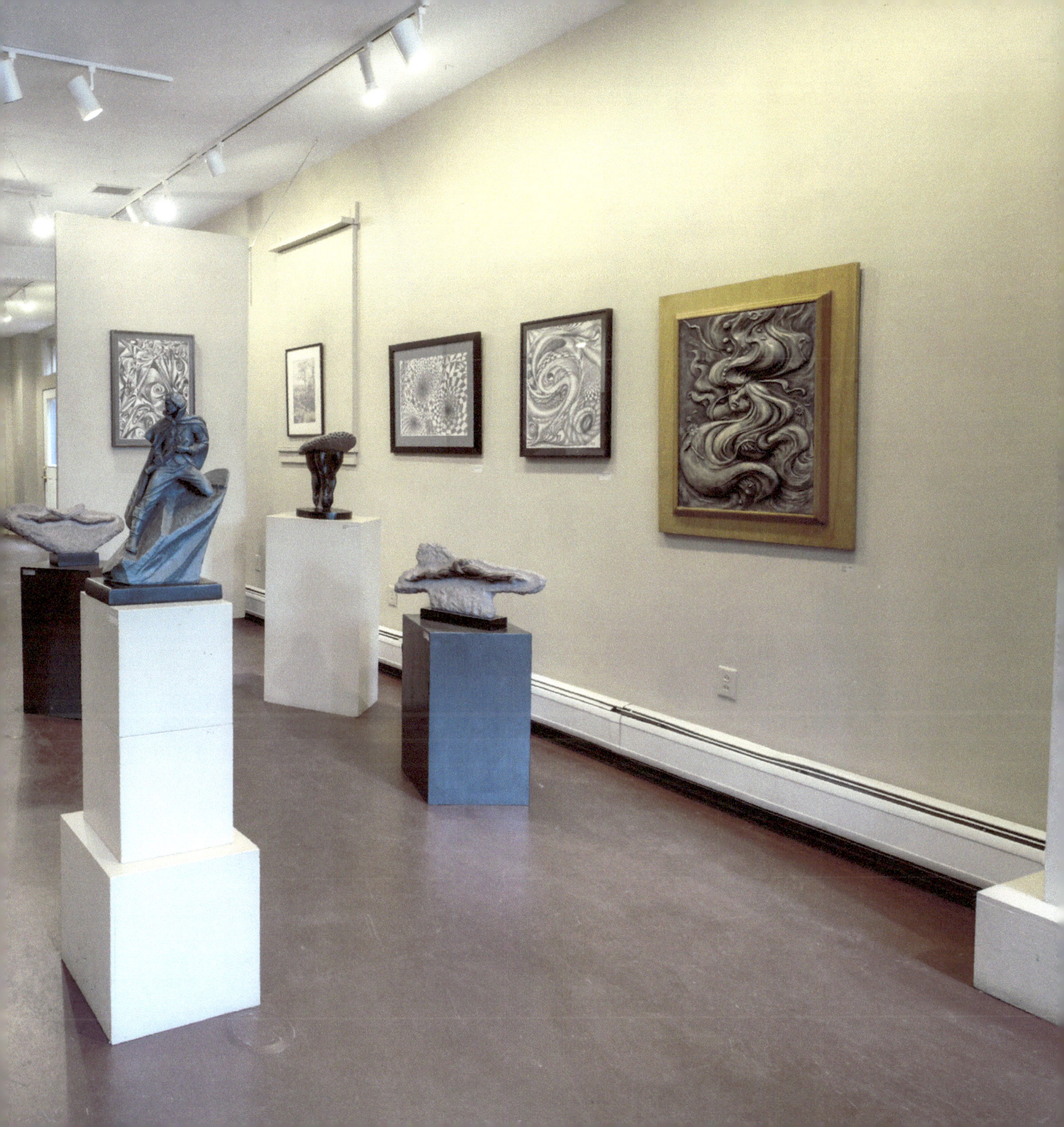

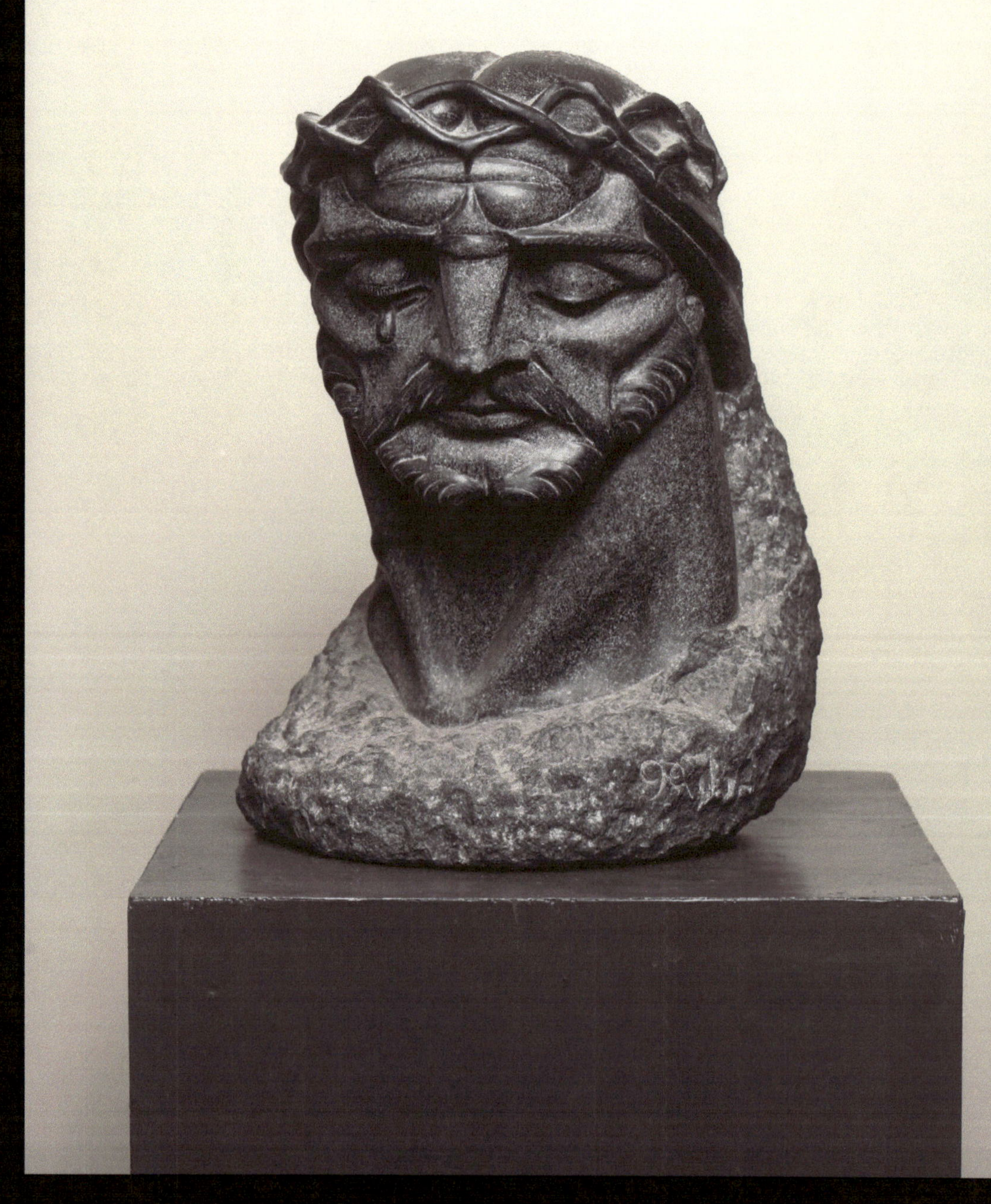

Christ Portrait 1979
black granite
16.25"h x 13"w x 11"d

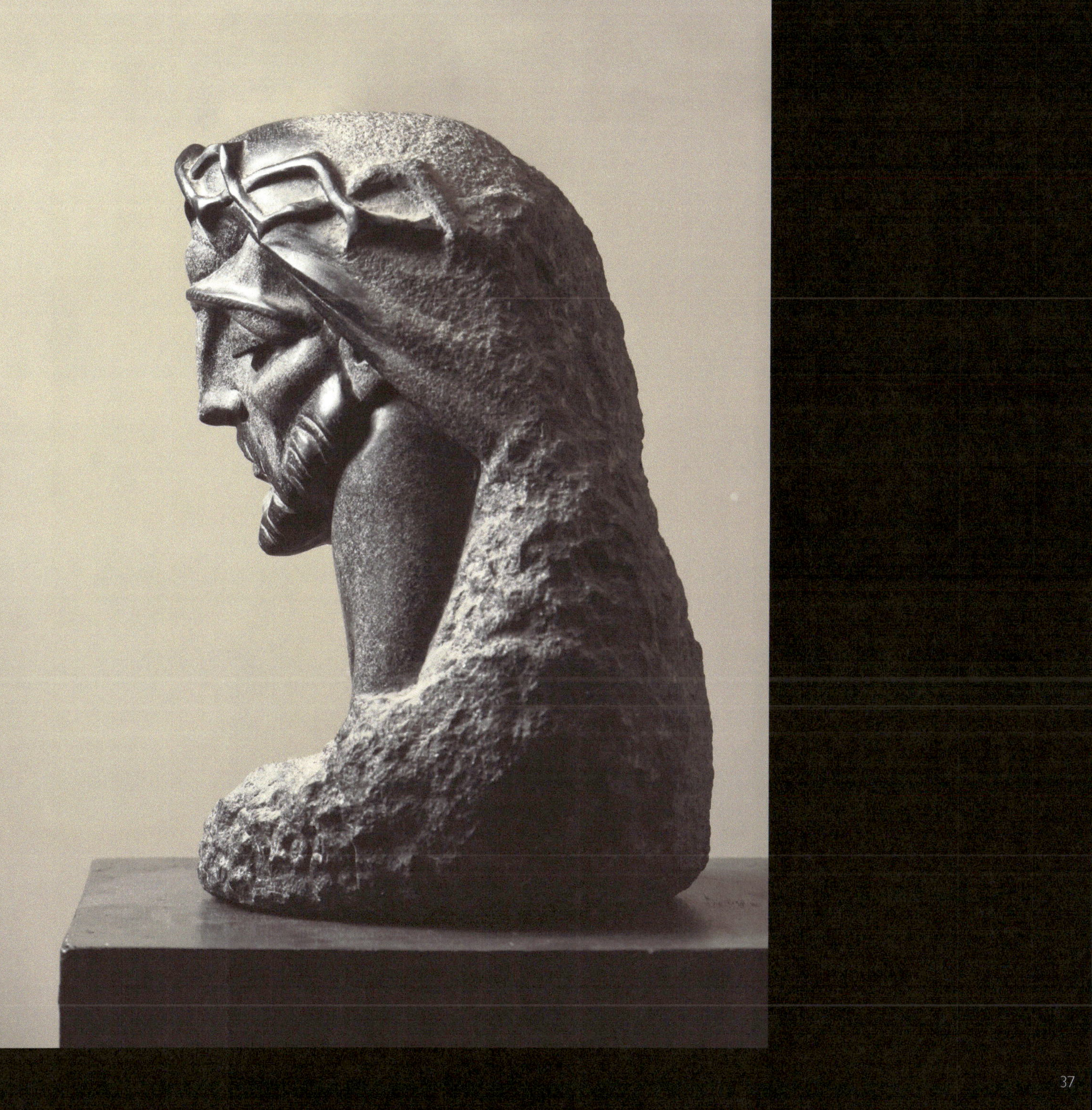

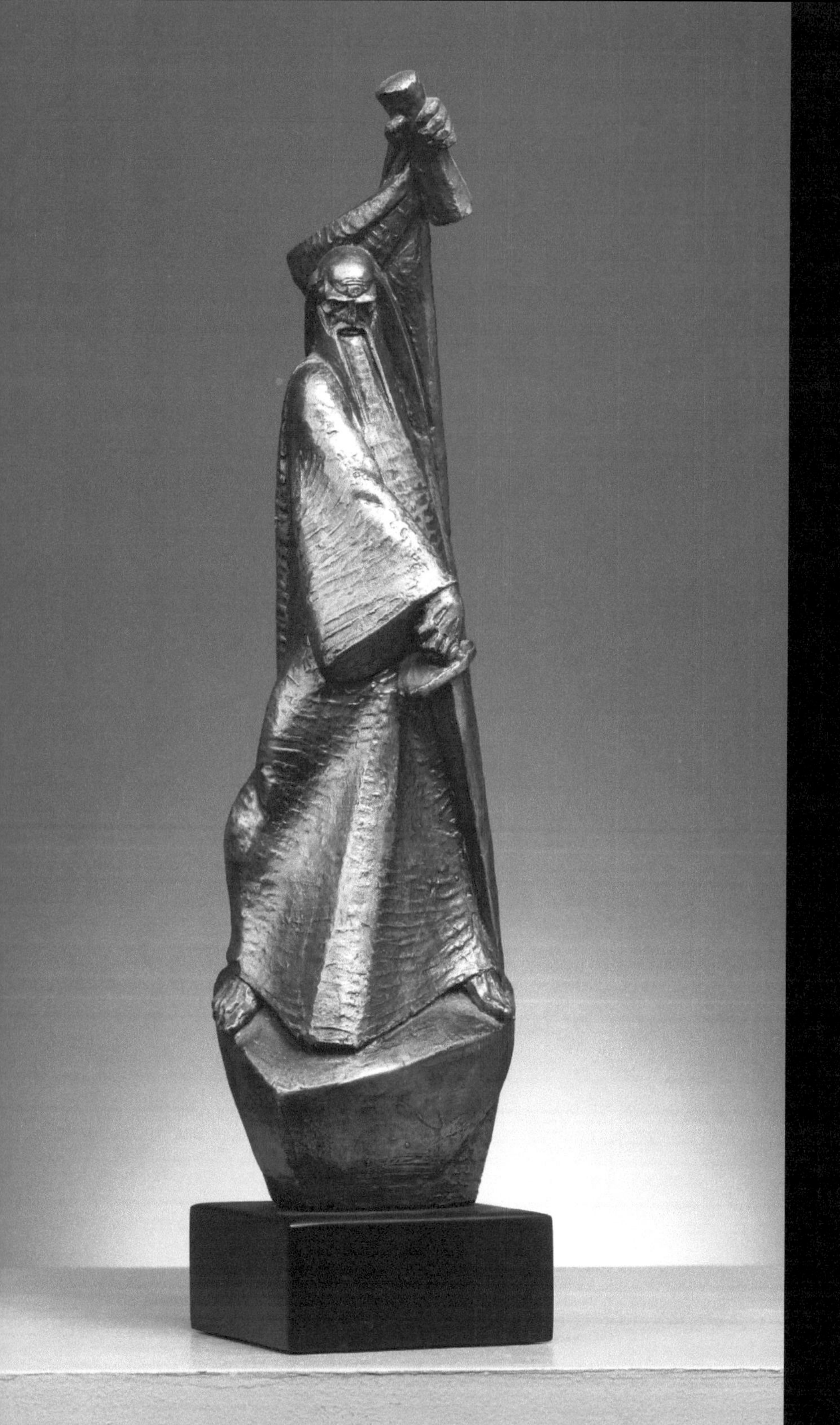

Saint Paul 1986
plaster
Collection of Giuliano Cecchinelli
21.5"h x 6.5"w x 6"d

Transfiguration 1988
resin
Collection of Fran Stoddard
16"h x 11"w x 11"d

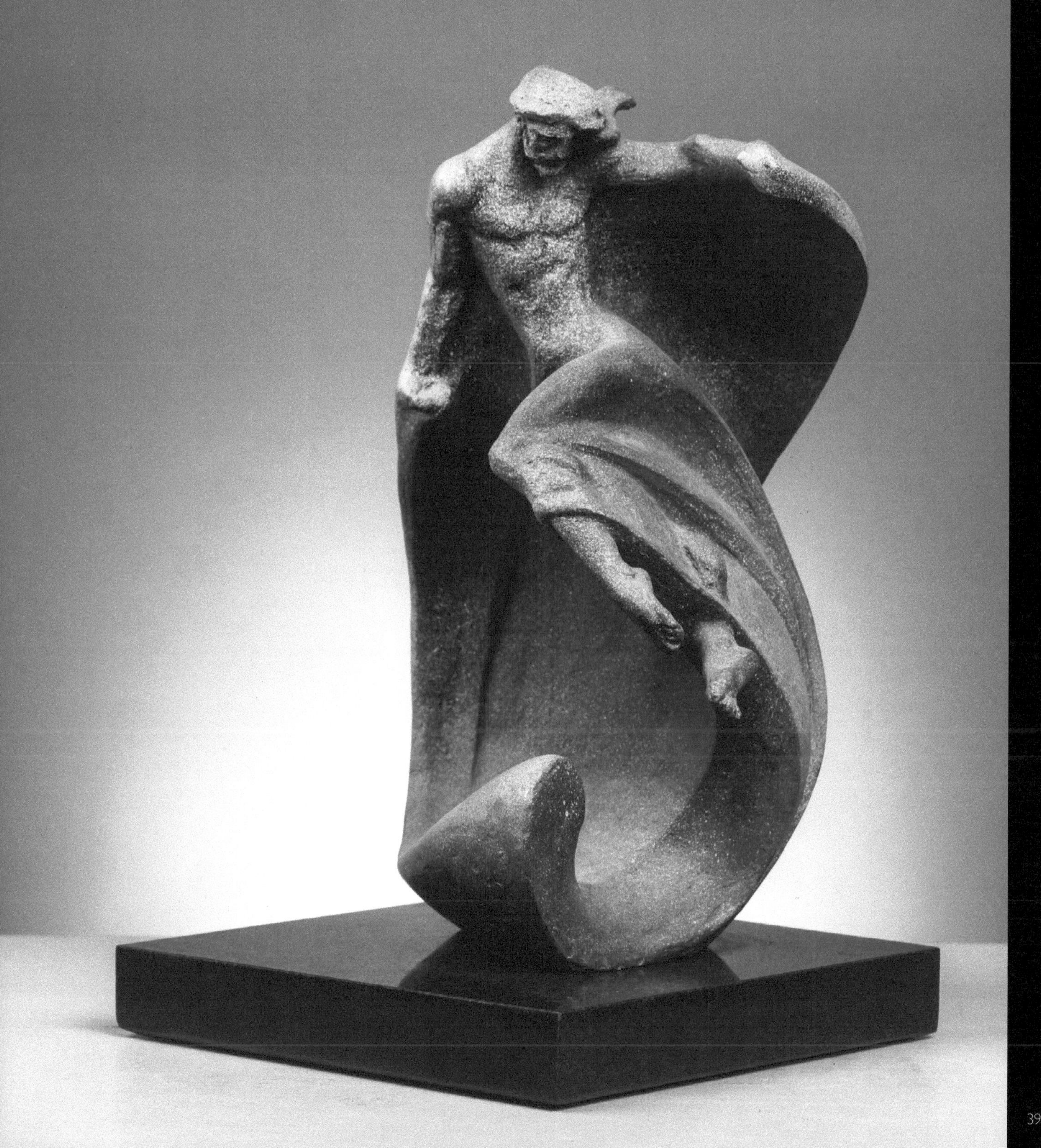

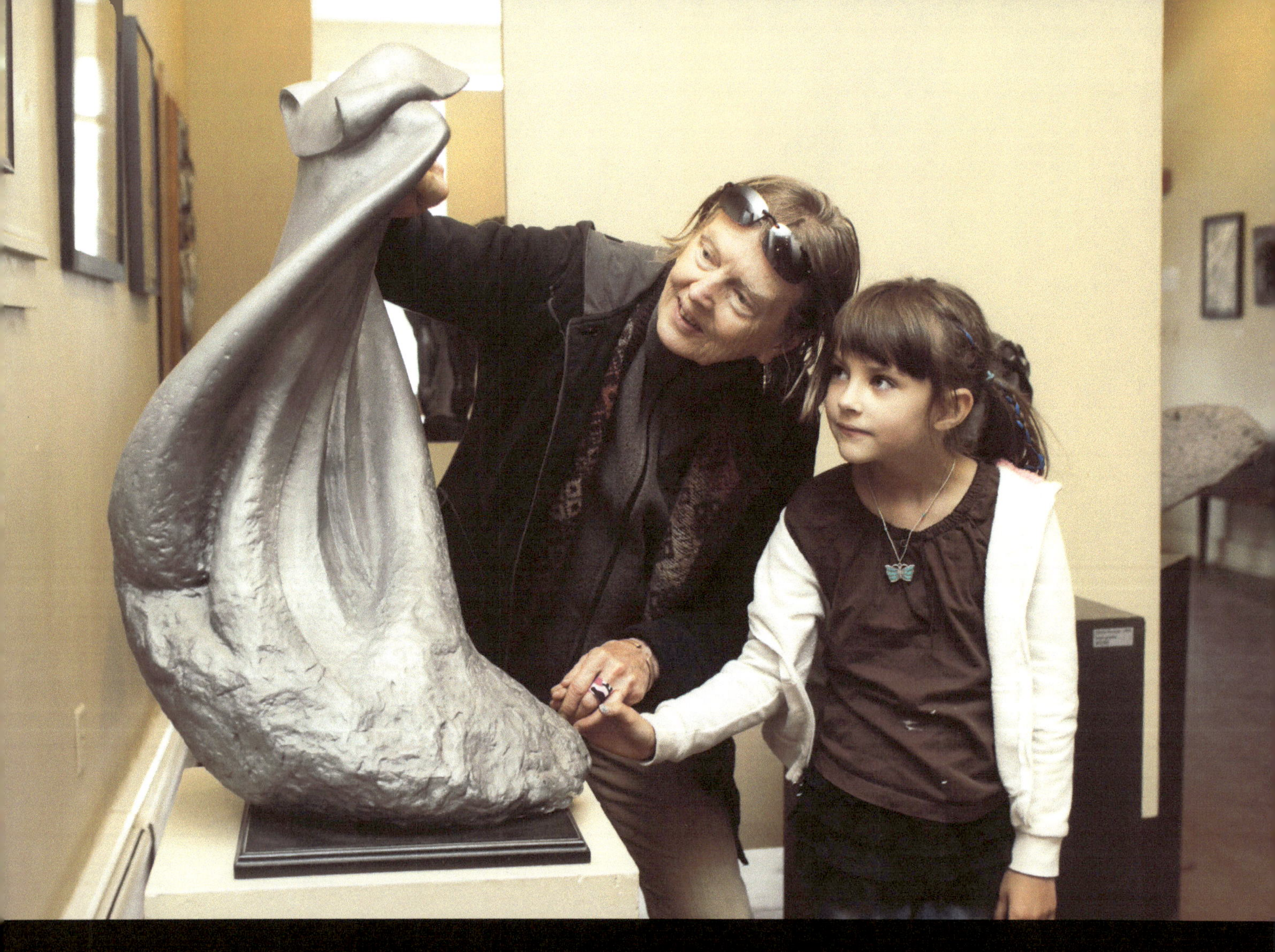

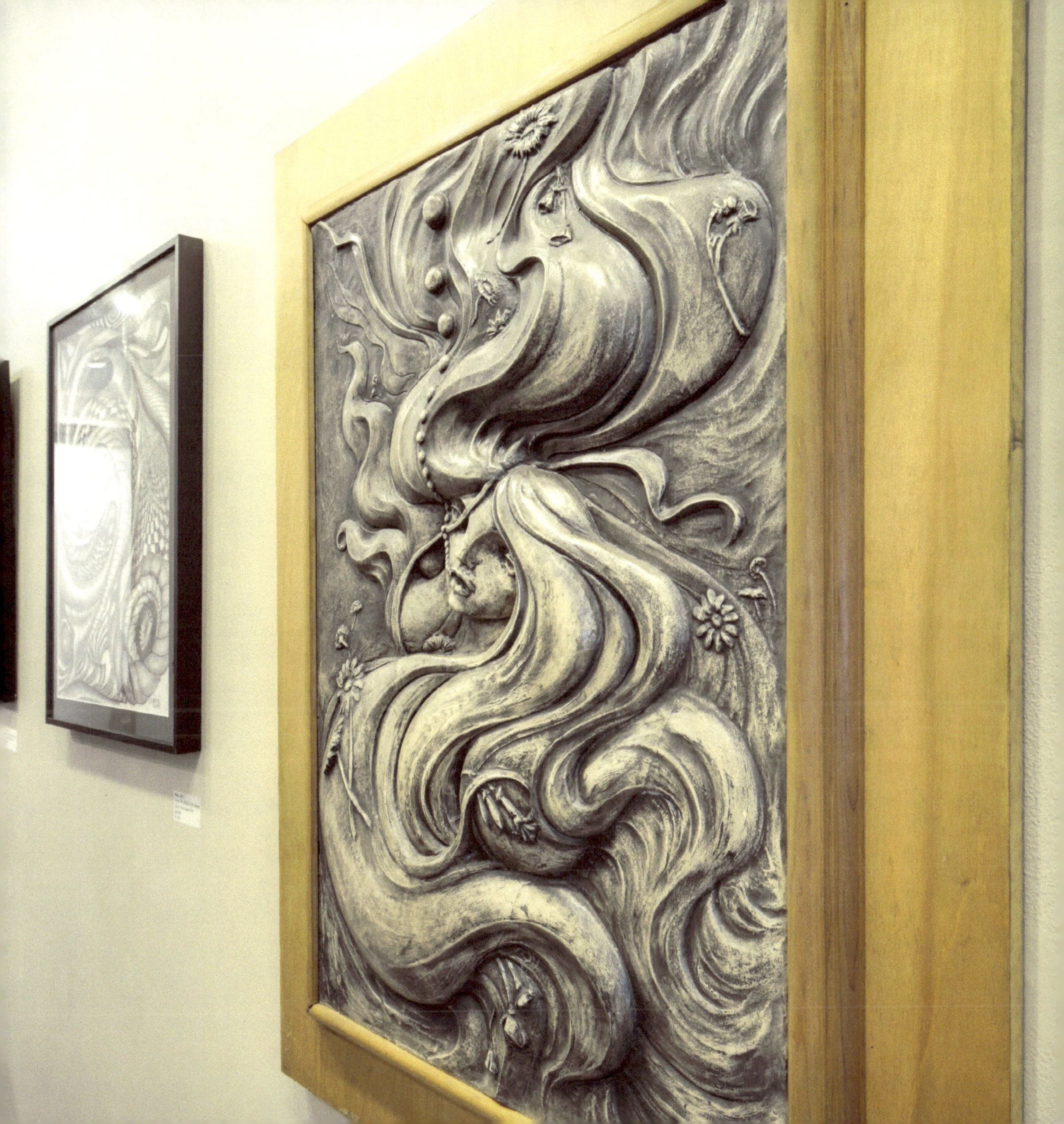

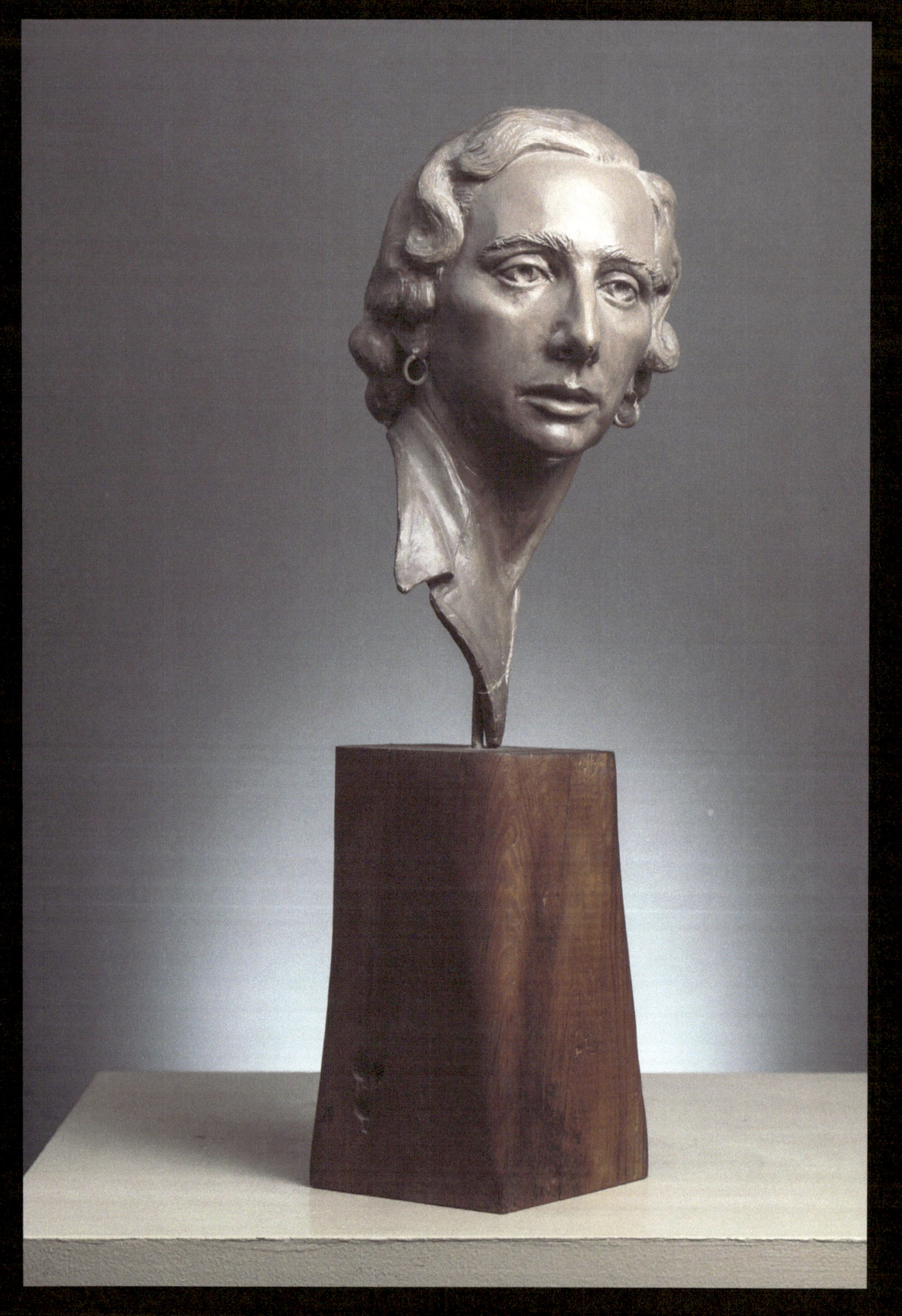

Aurora Galli 1952
plaster
courtesy of Aldrich Public Library, Barre
14.5"h x 9"w x 9"d

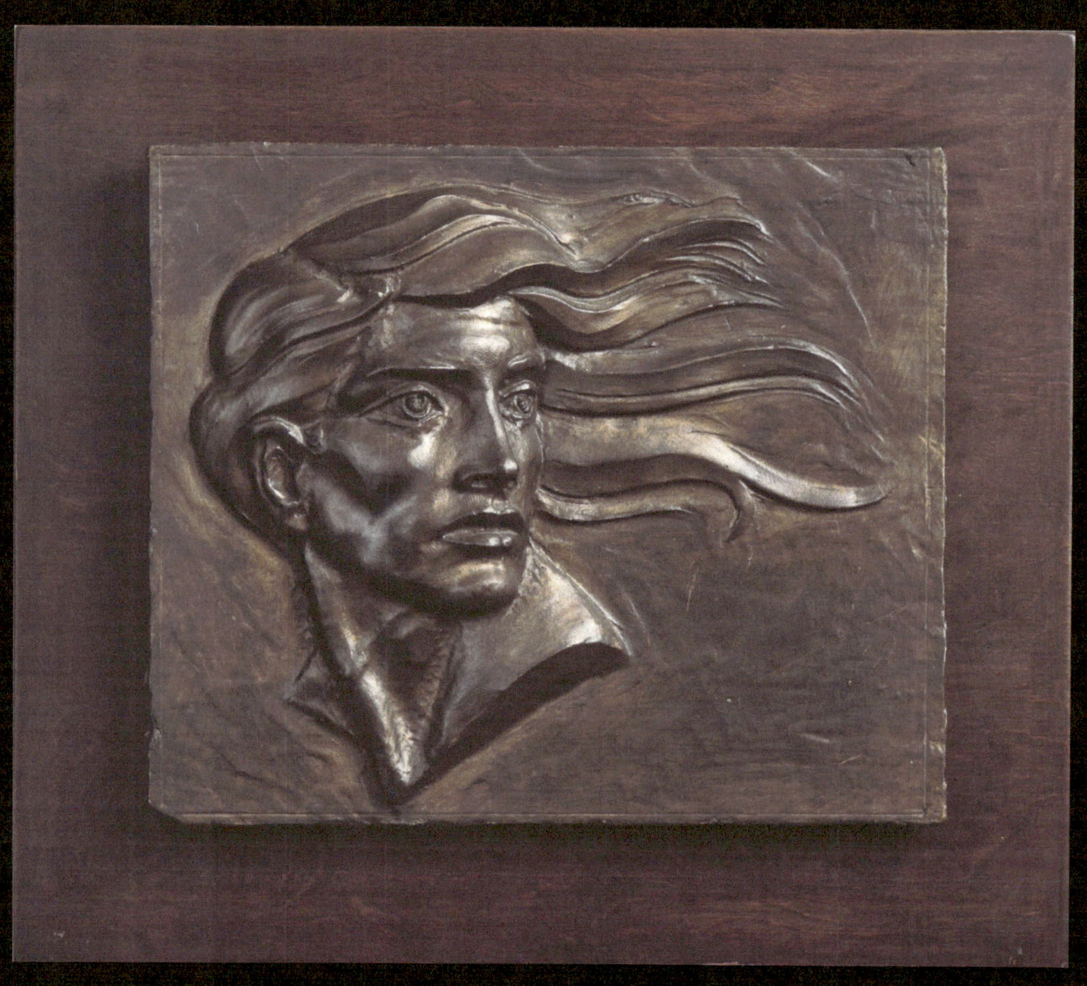

Bronze Patina Study (After a Sketch by Prud 'Hon) 1980
resin
Collection of Fran Stoddard
2.5" d x 13.25"w x 11"h

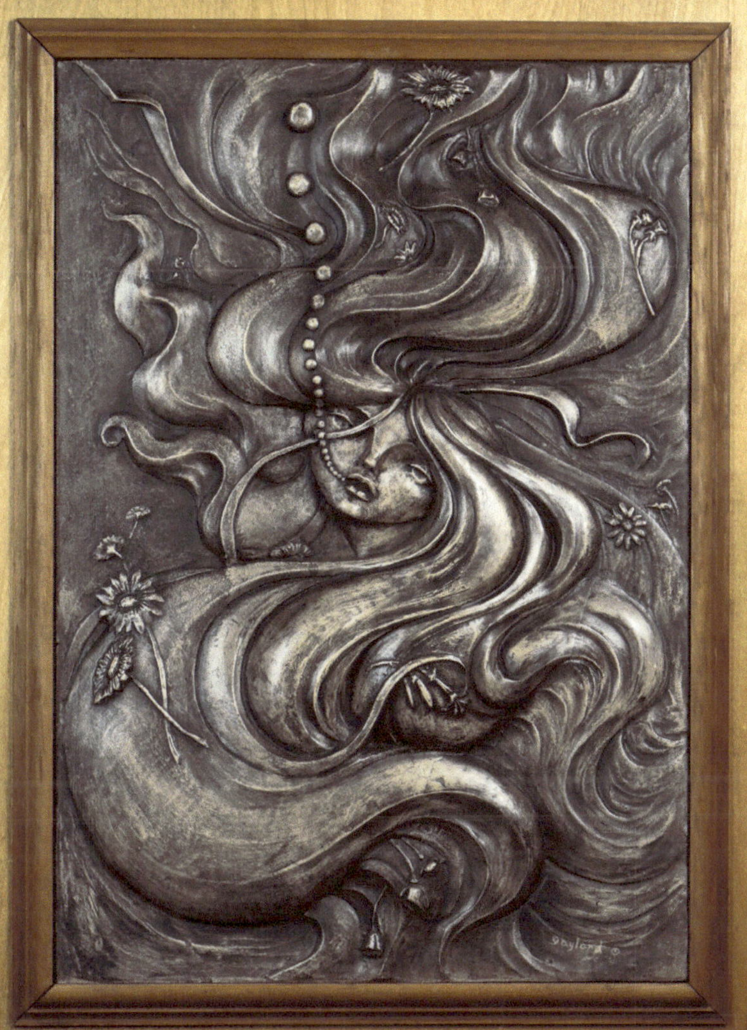

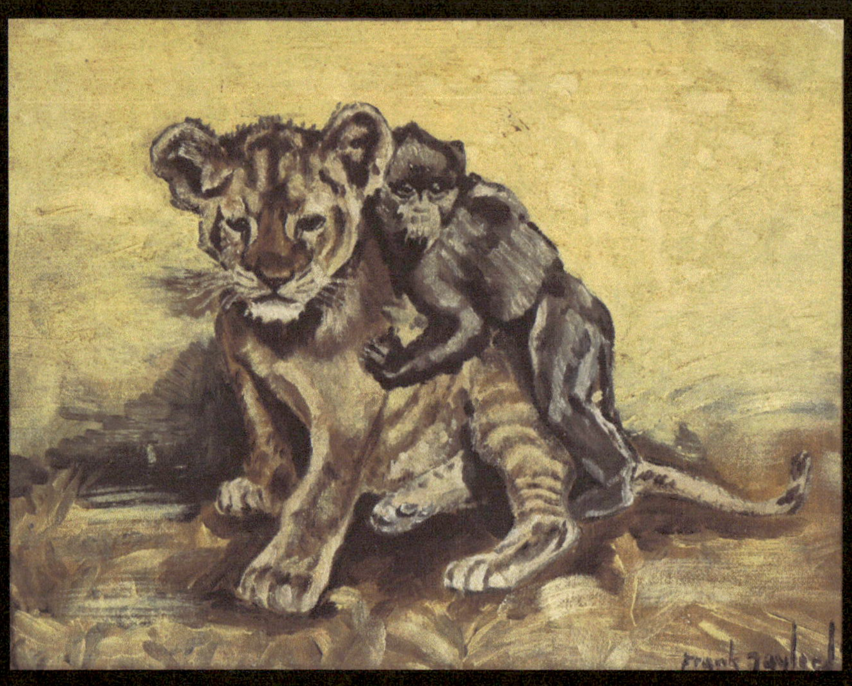

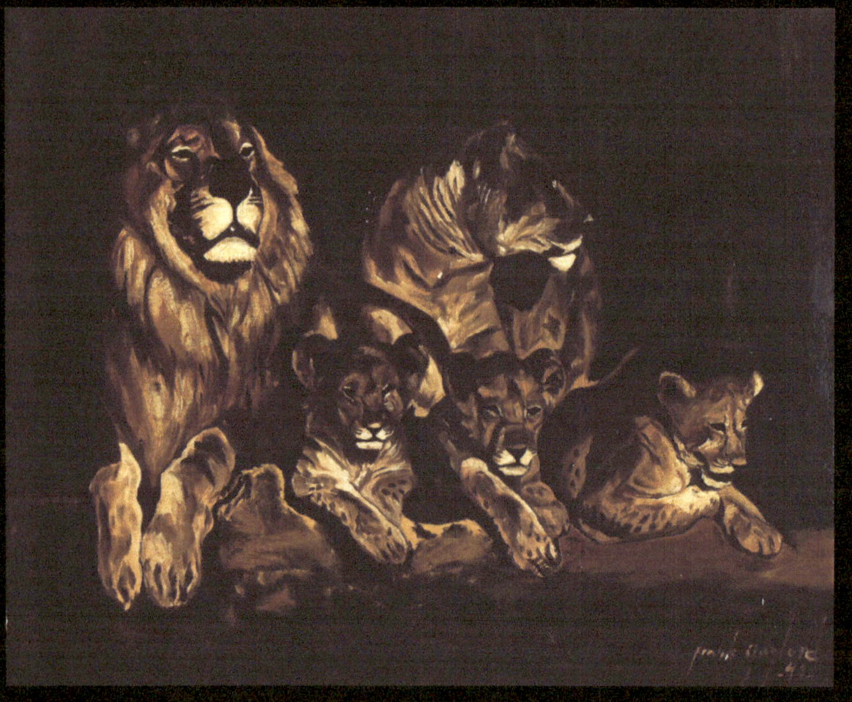

Lion and Monkey 1940
(Frank Gaylord was 15 yrs old)
oil
11.25" x 8.25"

Lion Family 1942
(Frank Gaylord was 17 yrs old)
oil
29.75" x 23"

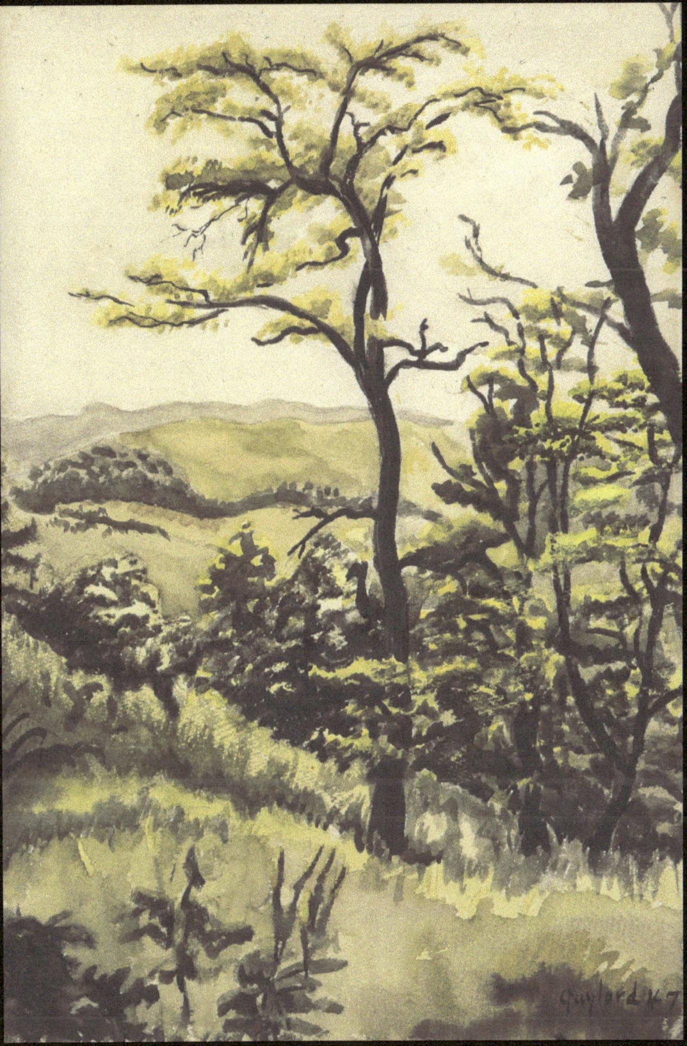

Untitled Landscape I 1946
watercolor
Collection of The Waskowmium

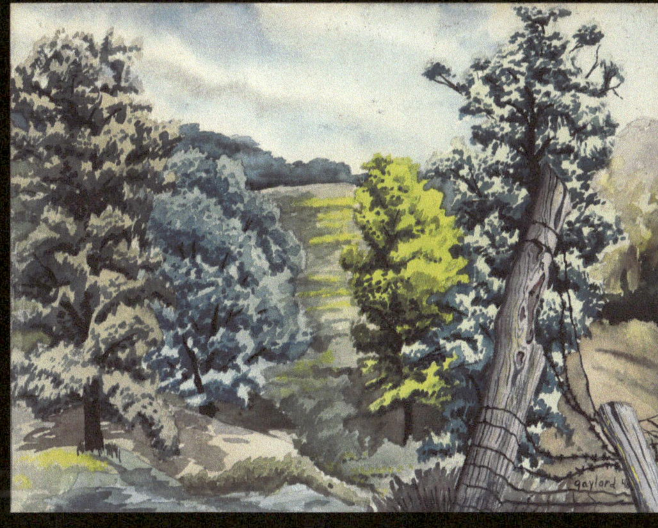

Untitled Landscape II 1948
watercolor
Collection of Giuliano Cecchinelli, II

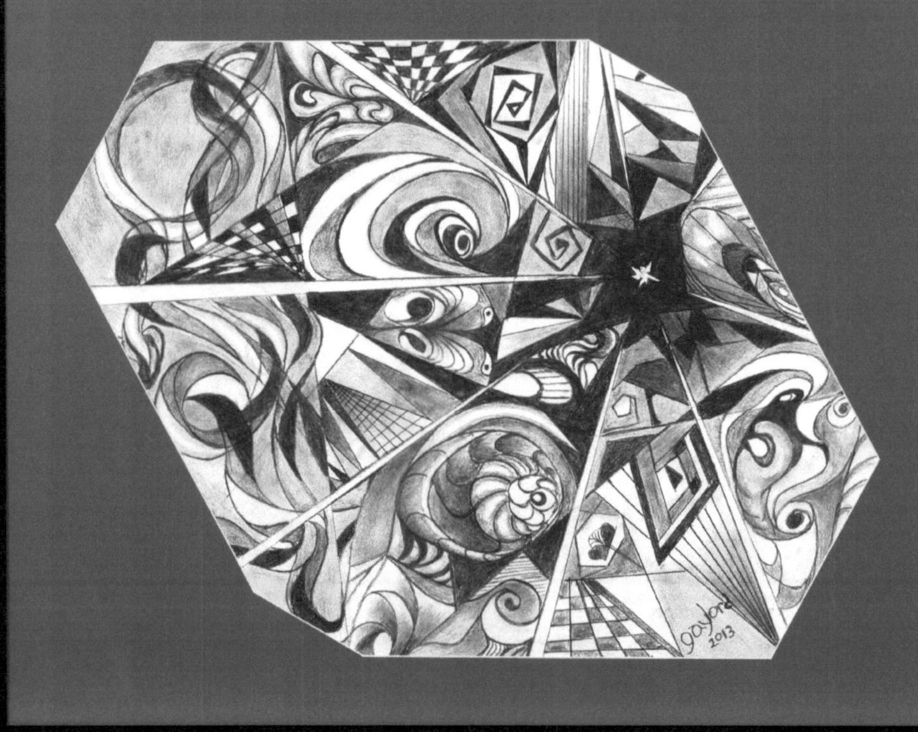

Annabelle 2013
From The GOGO Girls (Girls Once Gazed On) Series
graphite
23" x 16.25"

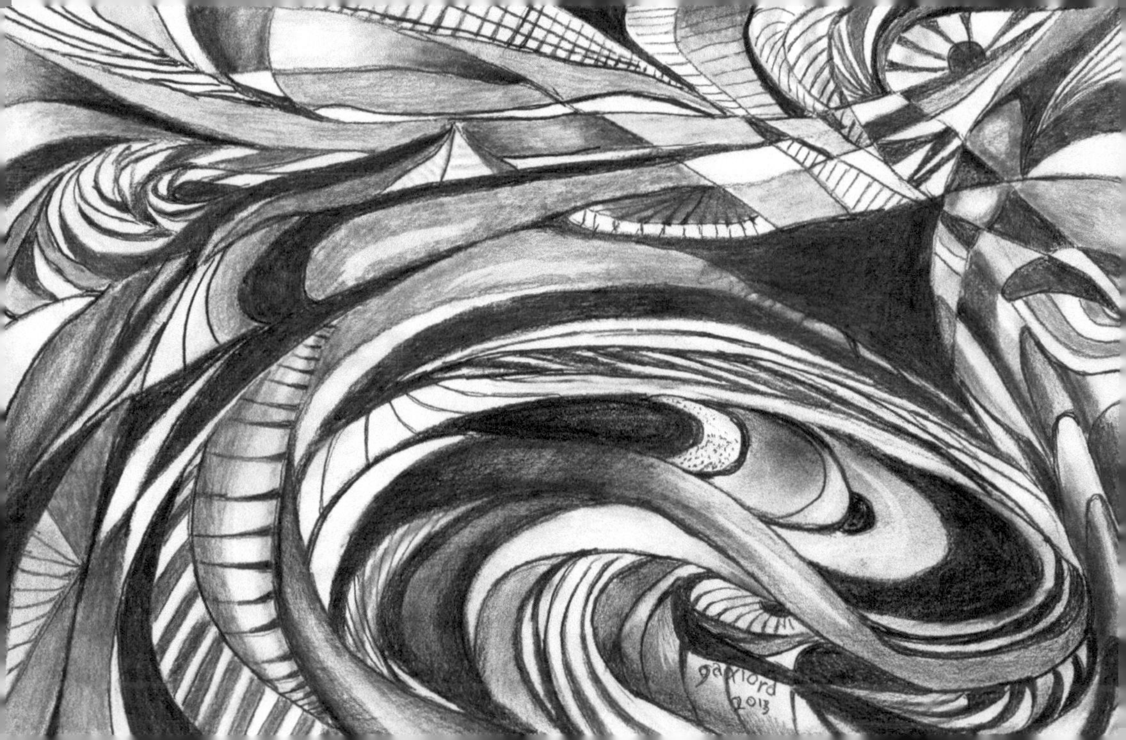
gaylord
2013

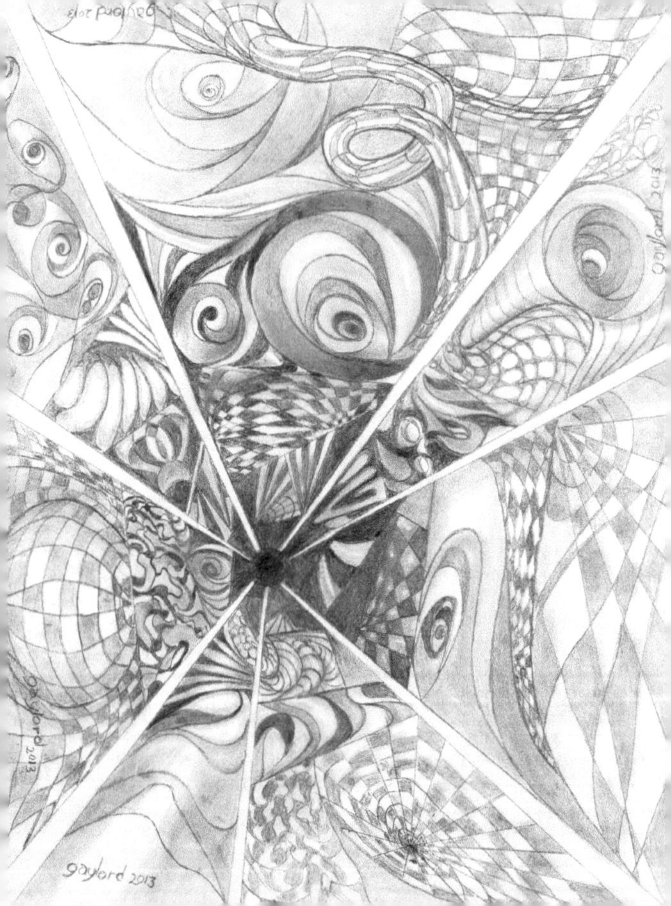
gaylord 2013

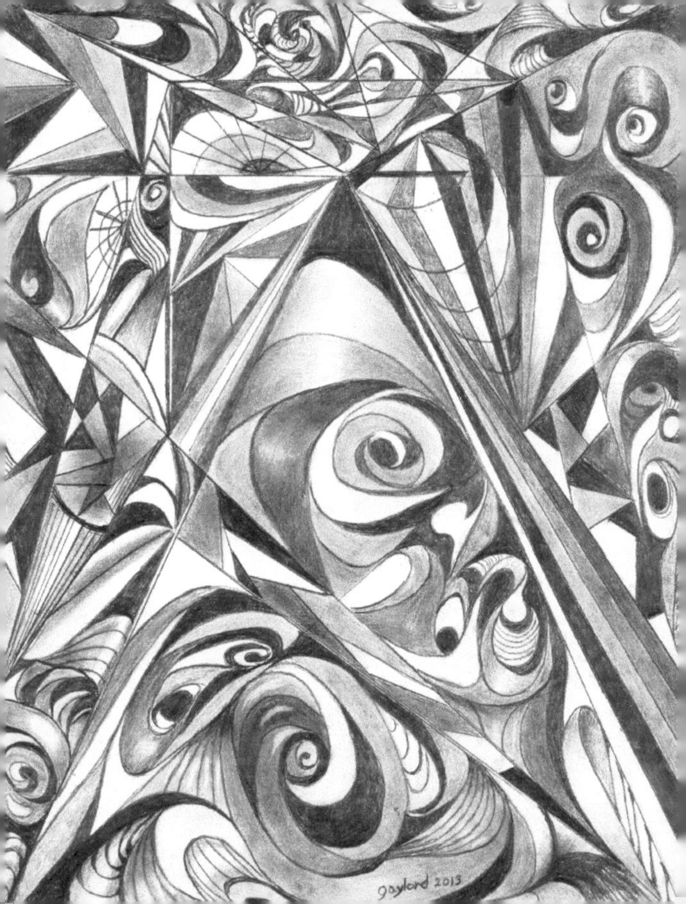
gaylord 2013

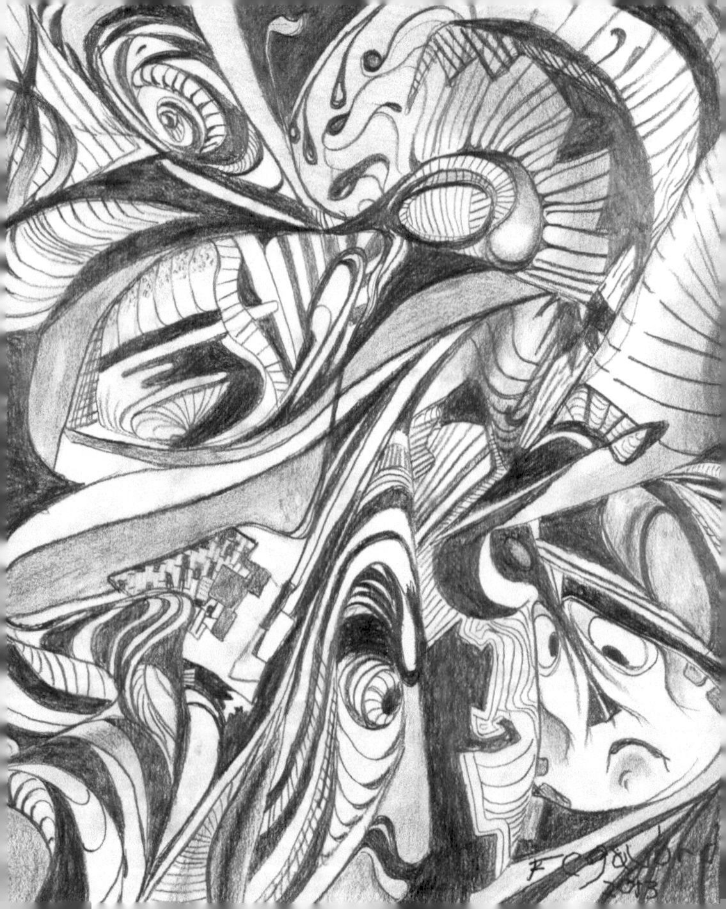

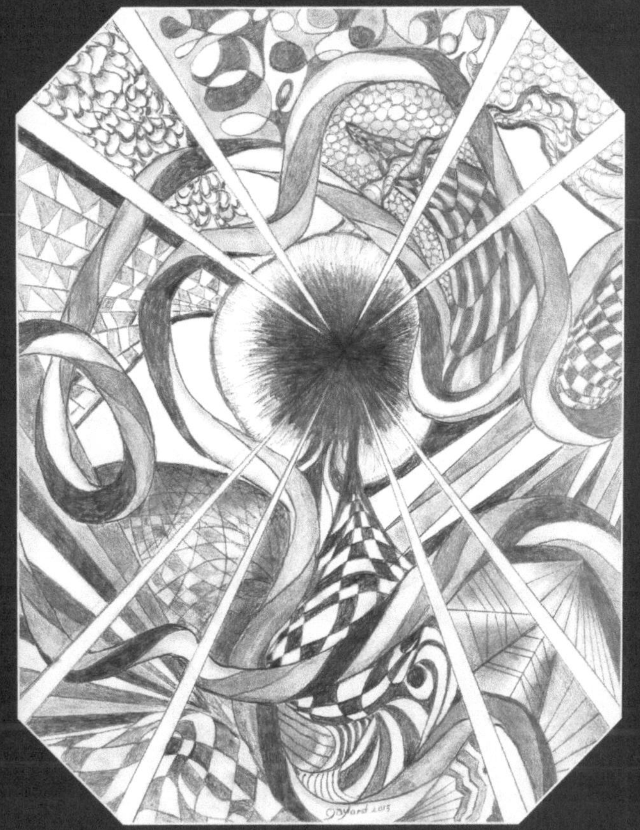

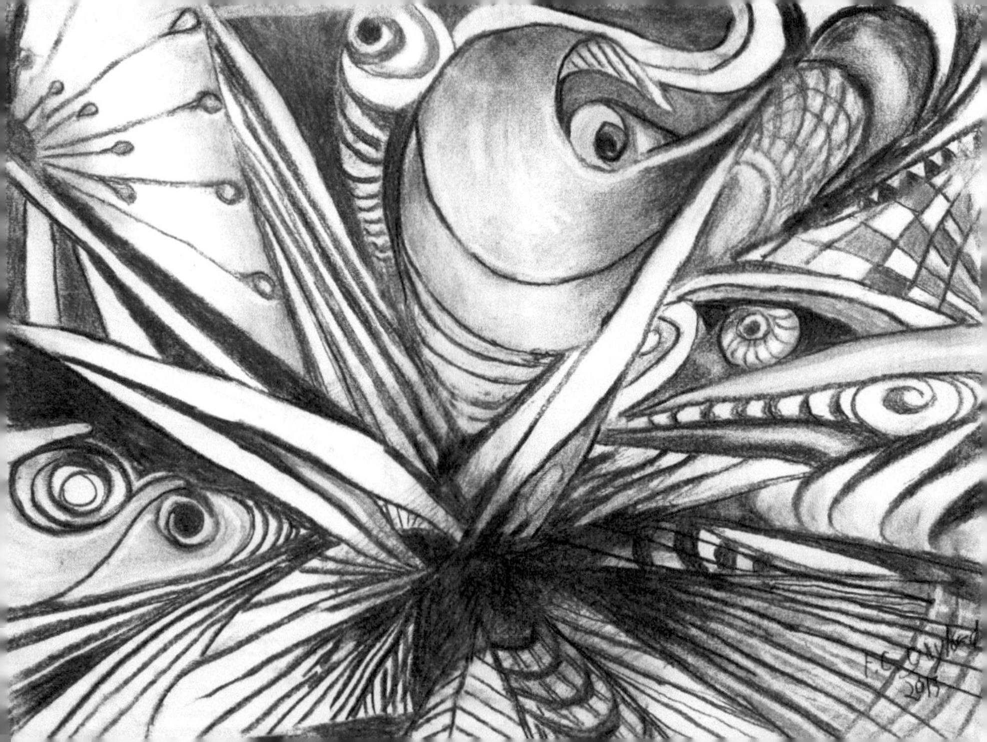
E. G. Gaylord
2013

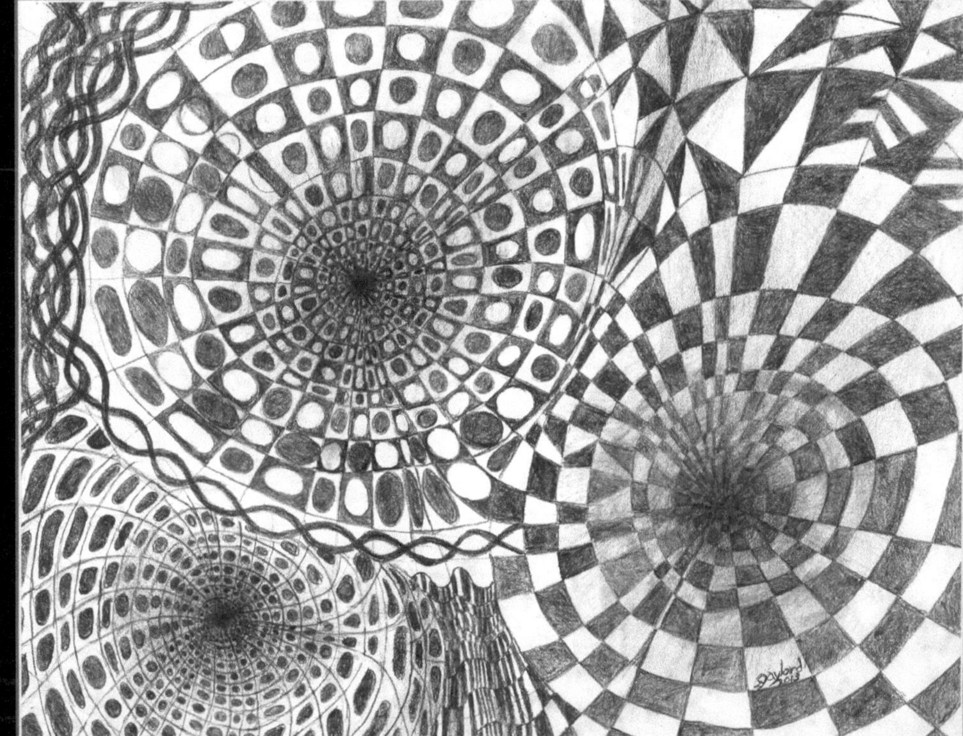
Gaylord
2013

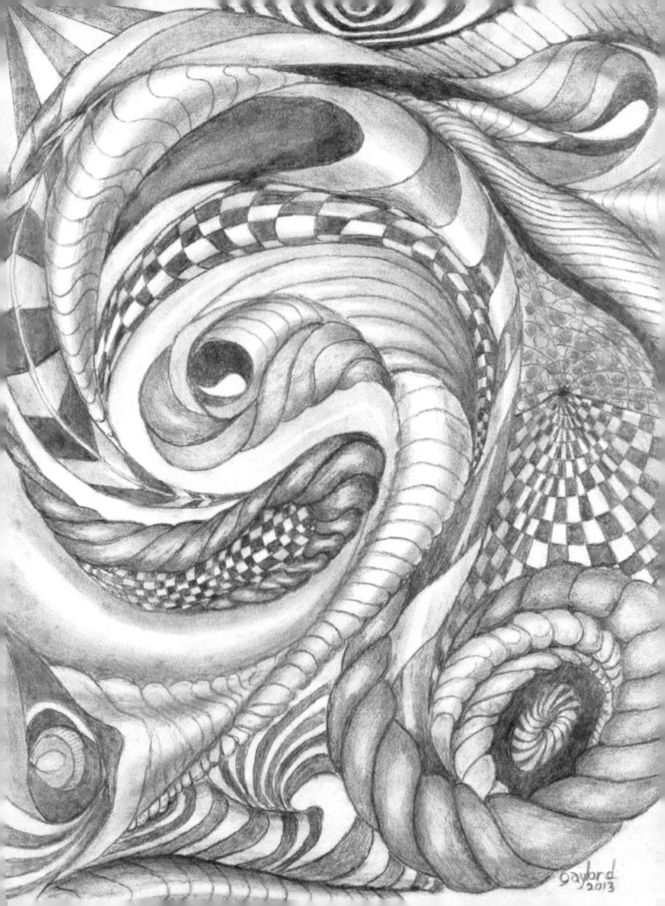
gaylord
2013

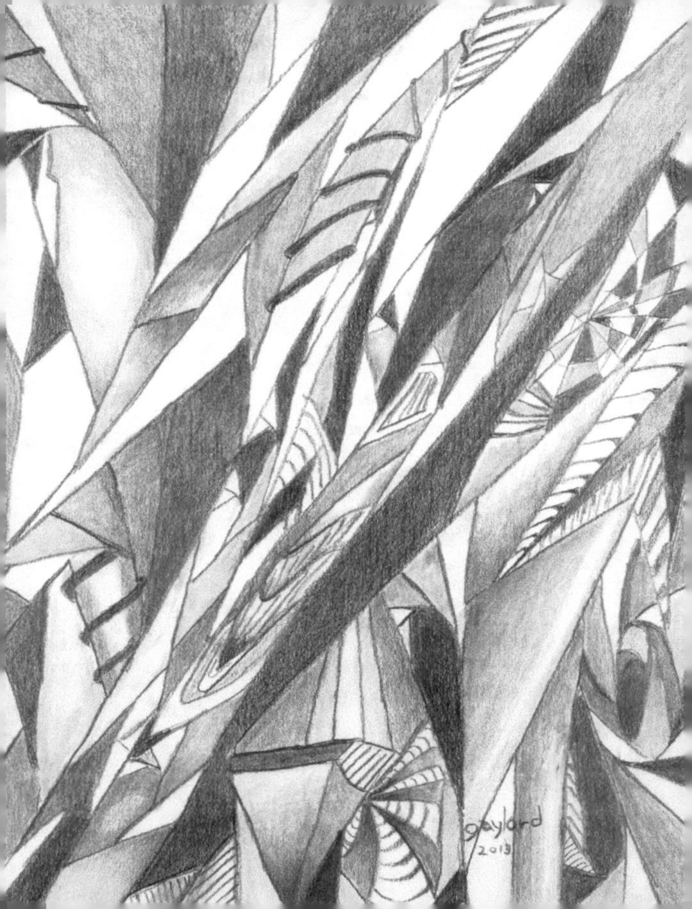
gaylord
2013

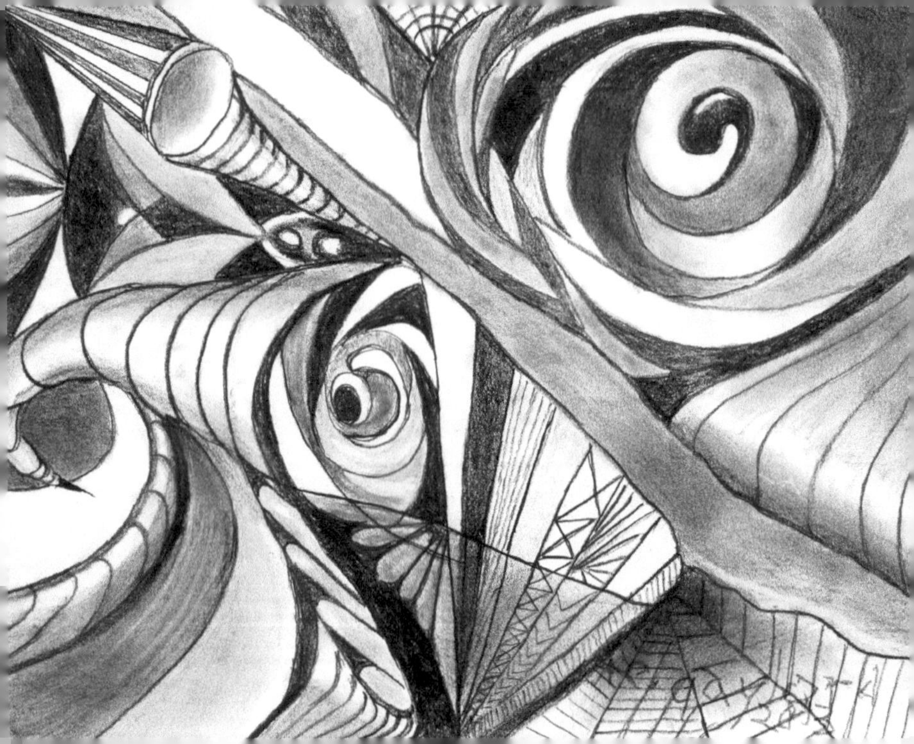

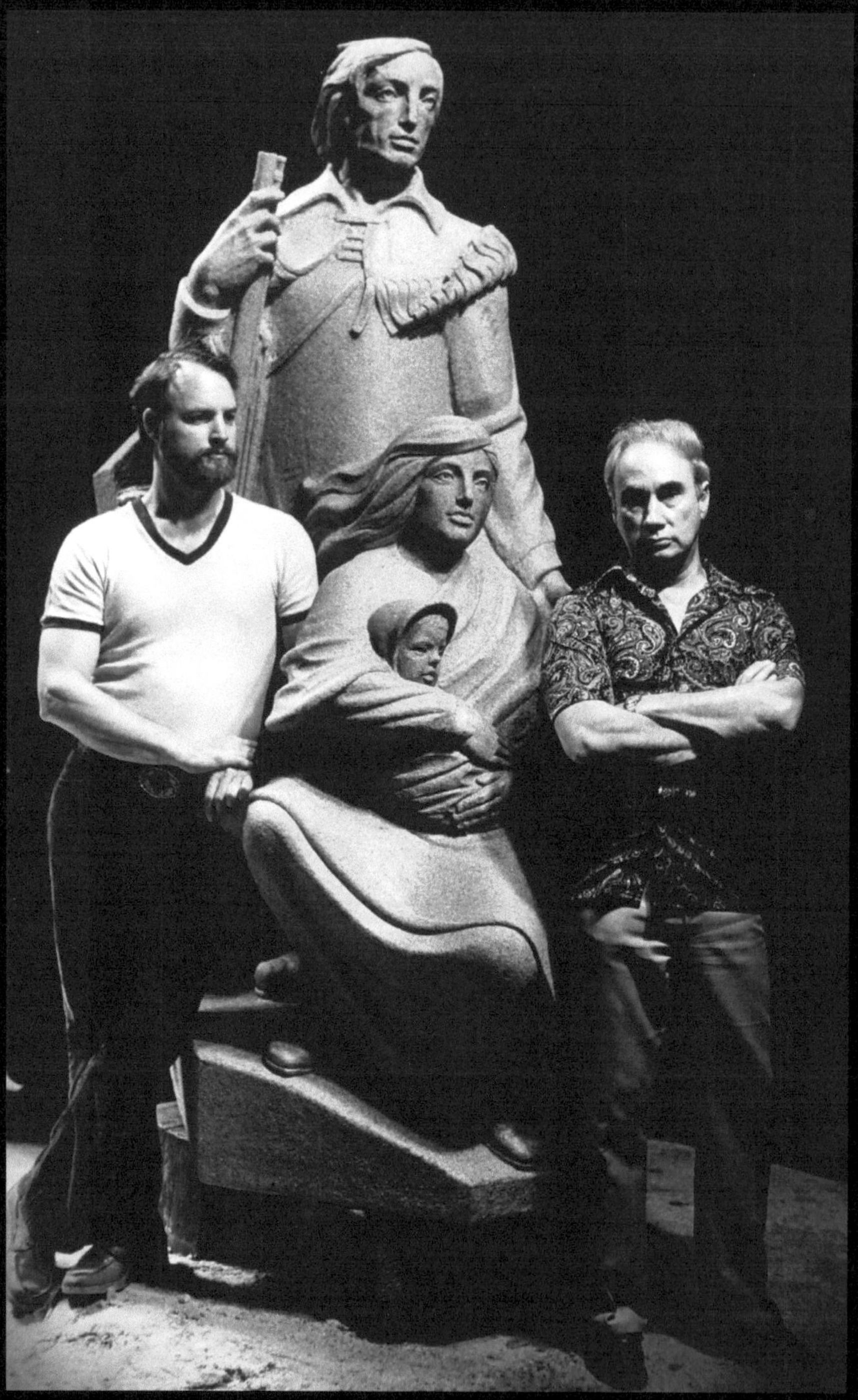

An historic image of John Hanna (1947–2008), on left, and Frank C. Gaylord, on right, standing with Pioneer Family, *a sculpture designed by Gaylord and carved by Hanna. It was erected in Akron, Ohio, in 1980. Photograph courtesy of the Hannas.*

www.ingramcontent.com/pod-product-compliance
Lightning Source LLC
LaVergne TN
LVHW070148110826
845147LV00002B/351

9780692666913